Praise for *American Resistance*

"Rothkopf, host of the invaluable *Deep State Radio* podcast, pays a long-overdue tribute to the 'deep state' that tried to keep Trump from doing more damage. In the process, he offers a powerful corrective to the negative stereotypes of 'bureaucrats' that are all too deeply rooted in American culture. Even if you remember all the Trump scandals he chronicles (there are so many!), you will feel outrage all over again reading this book—along with gratitude to all the dedicated public servants who tried to do the right thing and shared their stories with Rothkopf."

—**MAX BOOT**, columnist, *Washington Post*, and senior fellow, the Council on Foreign Relations

"One of the biggest debates during the Trump years concerned those who went to work for him in all branches of the government. Were they serving the public by 'saving' the country from the worst of Trump's excesses? Or were they ambitious careerists taking the jobs available while pretending that their service was in the nation's best interests? Rothkopf's fascinating, well-written, and carefully researched book is essential reading for those interested in how the 'deep state' performed in the Trump years—a topic that could well become worryingly relevant again."

—**ROBERT KAGAN**, senior fellow, the Brookings Institution, and author of *The Jungle Grows Back*

"Rothkopf has been a strong and thoughtful critic of Trumpism from the start because he cares passionately about democratic institutions. *American Resistance* turns the idea of the 'deep state' on its head, using it to describe the committed civil servants and policy experts who—imperfectly, but also, in key moments, courageously—worked to block or disrupt some of Trump's most dangerous initiatives. Rothkopf's provocative insight: the deep state is often the last line of defense against the dark state."

—**E.J. DIONNE JR.**, coauthor of *100% Democracy* and *One Nation After Trump*

"With an almost unparalleled knowledge of the inner workings of our government, Rothkopf has written a sobering and at times harrowing account not simply of how bad things were but of how much worse they could have been . . . during the Trump Administration. *American Resistance* is much more, and much more important than, a postmortem of the Trump years. Exhaustively researched and bolstered by eye-opening interviews with dozens of experts and former government officials, Rothkopf's book offers a clarion call for us to remain vigilant against anti-democratic forces and a long-overdue tribute to the often-maligned civil servants who saved us from the worst administration in modern history. In a very crowded field, what Rothkopf has written is not just compelling, it is essential."

—**MARY L. TRUMP**, clinical psychologist and author
of *Too Much and Never Enough* and *The Reckoning*

"This deeply researched and finely written story of the Trump presidency functions as the ultimate political cautionary tale. Rothkopf has spent much of his life sailing the treacherous waters of Washington, and in *American Resistance*, he brings a sharply observed set of sensible observations and timely prescriptions to help us navigate the roiling waters of our dangerously turbulent republic. A necessary and riveting book."

—**ADMIRAL JAMES STAVRIDIS**, US Navy (Ret.),
former supreme allied commander, NATO

"Rothkopf has written the Trump administration story that needs to be told: how close we came to losing our democracy and the public servants who saved us. In *American Resistance: The Inside Story of How the Deep State Saved the Nation*, Rothkopf expertly explains how the much maligned 'deep state' is actually a cohort of steadfast professionals committed to honoring the oaths they took to uphold the Constitution. This book offers essential insights into a vitally important world too few understand or appreciate."

—**LT. COL. ALEXANDER VINDMAN**, US Army (Ret.),
author of *Here, Right Matters*

AMERICAN
RESISTANCE

AMERICAN RESISTANCE

The Inside Story
of How the Deep State
Saved the Nation

DAVID ROTHKOPF

PUBLICAFFAIRS

New York

PublicAffairs
Hachette Book Group
1290 Avenue of the Americas, New York, NY 10104
www.publicaffairsbooks.com
@Public_Affairs
Printed in the United States of America
First Edition: November 2022

Published by PublicAffairs, an imprint of Perseus Books, LLC, a subsidiary of Hachette Book Group, Inc. The PublicAffairs name and logo is a trademark of the Hachette Book Group.

The Hachette Speakers Bureau provides a wide range of authors for speaking events. To find out more, go to www.hachettespeakersbureau.com or call (866) 376-6591.

The publisher is not responsible for websites (or their content) that are not owned by the publisher.

Editorial production by Christine Marra, Marrathon Production Services. www.marrathoneditorial.org
Print book interior design by Jane Raese.
Set in 12-point Adobe Caslon

Library of Congress Cataloging-in-Publication Data has been applied for.
ISBNs: 9781541700635 (hardcover), 9781541700659 (ebook)

LSC-C

Printing 1, 2022

For Carla, Joanna and Brad, Laura and Aaron,
and for my loyal research assistant, Grizzly

"Wherever Law ends, Tyranny begins."

—JOHN LOCKE, 1690

Contents

A Word of Thanks
to the Deep State

Ring the bells that still can ring.

—LEONARD COHEN, "ANTHEM"

I THINK THERE ARE few places in the world as misunderstood as Washington, DC.

You would think that given all the coverage Washington gets in the news, all the times it has been depicted in film, television, and novels, the world would better understand its nature.

But it suits many in our political classes and in the media, and among both our friends and rivals overseas, to depict Washington, and in particular the large part of Washington engaged in the business of the government of the United States, as a caricature.

Some of the descriptions are more or less benign and only mildly derisive. John F. Kennedy, for example, borrowed a line originally spoken by Senator Warren Magnuson (of Washington, the state), when he described the capital as a "city of southern efficiency and northern charm." The humorist P. J. O'Rourke cut a little closer to the bone and to the tone of more mainstream characterizations when he said: "The mystery of government is not how Washington works but how to make it stop."

For most of my lifetime, however, I have listened and watched as politicians from both parties argued that their greatest qualification for assuming a leadership role in Washington was how anti-Washington or un-Washington they were. It was a strange message. Donald Trump ran for president by arguing that he had no Washington experience, was not part of the "Washington establishment." He was far from the first to do so. In fact, since Jimmy Carter ran for president in 1976, the candidate best able to present themselves as a Washington outsider has won every single election but one. (And even then, in 1988 George H. W. Bush—son of a senator, a former member of Congress, party chief, CIA director, and vice president— tried to depict his opponent, Massachusetts governor Michael Dukakis, as a member of the eastern liberal "establishment.")

Why? The simplest explanation is that public trust in government has plummeted over the past sixty-five years. According to the Pew national election study, in 1958, 75 percent of Americans said they trusted the government. In the most recent version of the same poll, in 2021 that number was 24 percent. That is quite a collapse. So we must ask to what degree trust in government has fallen because government has been failing the people, because of gridlock, or because it has been too partisan? And how much of its fall has been because attacking government as being the problem has been a staple of politics, particularly on the Republican side of the aisle, since the 1980s?

In 1981 Ronald Reagan said that in the face of the economic crisis the country was confronting at that time, "Government is not the solution to our problem; government is the problem." Today, as low as the overall level of trust in government is nationwide, among members of the GOP it is much lower still. Only 9 percent of Republicans, or those leaning Republican, trust the government in Washington to do what is right compared to 36 percent of Democrats.

As much of that distrust as may be due to the hypocrisy, corruption, and incompetence of elected officials, a substantial amount of it has historically been directed at the "permanent government"—the bureaucracy. Again, politicians have run against that bureaucracy throughout America's modern era. Kennedy denigrated Eisenhower as a paper-pusher, implying he was consumed by the business of the bureaucracy. Nixon characterized bureaucrats as the principal obstacle to change in Washington. More recently, Newt Gingrich reflected how those arguments have evolved when he said: "We are at a crossroads. Down one road is a European centralized bureaucratic socialist welfare system in which politicians and bureaucrats define the future. Down the other road is proud, solid reaffirmation of American exceptionalism."

Most recently, the animus of the anti-government crowd has been directed at something characterized as the "deep state." The idea was that the bureaucracy was too large, too powerful, and that it did not answer to voters. The implication was that therefore it was a threat to democracy.

The idea of a "deep state" or something like it has been with us since the dawn of history. Even in the era of monarchs, the influence of courtiers or the clergy was watched suspiciously. In the days just after the American Revolution, rumors swirled about the influence of a secret society made up of Revolutionary War officers, known as the Society of the Cincinnati. Originally convened as a club to help preserve the fellowship these officers felt and to commemorate their contributions to the new country, critics worried about their influence. When it happened that the group met in Philadelphia at the same time as the Constitutional Convention, those suspicions rose. They were not diminished when the head of the society, George Washington, became the first president of the United States and other members, like Alexander Hamilton and the society's founder Henry Knox, entered his cabinet.

Later in history, the idea of a deep state became associated with everything from a secret network of military officers and civilians who sought to advance the ideology of Kemal Ataturk within the post–World War I Turkish government, to post–World War II concerns of such a group pulling the strings within the US national security community.

The most recent incarnation of the term "deep state" dates back at least a decade before Trump. It flowed from an idea floated by a second-string academic to the *Infowars* show of right-wing cheerleader Alex Jones, and then on to a 2016 book called *The Deep State: The Fall of the Constitution and the Rise of a Shadow Government* by a former congressional staffer named Mike Lofgren. Lofgren argued that he was, according to an NPR profile of him, not a conspiracy theorist. Instead, he made the case that "big institutions, inside and outside of government, are so entrenched it is hard to bring any real change. Political options are limited." Whatever his rationale, the idea was a hit with the American right wing, and whereas there were "according to TV transcripts" only sixty-four mentions of the term on TV in 2016, by 2017 that number hit twenty-three hundred and doubled the following year. It was catnip to media outlets like Fox News and Breitbart and

Trumpists who saw in it a potential scapegoat that supported the right-wing's long-standing argument that government is part of the problem.

The popularity of such ideas—and there are many parallel but similar conspiracy theories, from those that warn of the influence of the Illuminati to those that assert the all-powerful nature of Freemasons or the world Jewish conspiracy—is due to the fact that they neatly explain to many in the public why they feel powerless. Alternatively, or in addition, such theories provide a useful target at which the frustrated may direct their anger. And invariably the conspiracy theories, as in the case of the deep state, are not just casual figments of overheated imaginations, but opportunities for mischief and more by people who use them to help gain power for themselves.

The general public in the United States has not been helped in discerning the real nature of their government in Washington from how it has been characterized by opportunistic politicians or the spinners of conspiracy theories. Nor has it been aided by the recent evolution of the media by which most Americans learn of what is going on in Washington. Once the FCC repealed the Fairness Doctrine in 1987, broadcasters no longer had to present opposing sides of important public issues. This was one among several factors that led to the growth of a new phenomenon: media franchises that catered to specific political groups with news and opinion designed to reinforce rather than simply report the facts, or challenge or broaden the views of the listeners.

From the growing popularity of radio shows like that of Alex Jones or Rush Limbaugh, to the birth of Rupert Murdoch's and Roger Ailes's Fox News in 1996, to the emergence of internet platforms built around the same premise (like Breitbart), the American population increasingly came to live in media bubbles. (More progressive outlets also emerged during this period, as well.) They listened to the news that described the world as they believed it was and featured analyses that supported their worldview.

The rise of these new media forms also contributed to deepening political polarization in the United States. This has been compounded by the fact that during the past forty years, the gap between America's haves and have-nots has grown. There are multiple metrics that show this. The incomes of the top one percent grew five times as fast as the incomes of the bottom 90 percent. According to a paper published by a Harvard researcher named Robert Manduca, whereas "in 1980 only about 12 percent of the population lived in places that were especially rich or especially poor, by 2013, it was over 30 percent." The ratio of income in the 90th percentile of income to that at the 10th percentile has grown from 9.1 in 1980 to 12.6 in 2018. Ninety percent of the gains following the Great Recession of 2008–2009 went to the top 10 percent of individuals.

At the same time as these gains were taking place, the role of money in politics was changing. With the Citizens United Supreme Court ruling in 2010, it was determined that money in politics could not be regulated as before, thus enabling the richest Americans and big corporations to spend far more (because they had far more) on political campaigns than average Americans. This bought influence that in exchange produced changes in the tax code and corporate regulations that enabled those with the most to carve out an even bigger piece of the economic pie, and thus gain more power. As far as representative democracy was concerned, it was a vicious cycle. ("Less government" is a slogan that often meant "more for me" for those who were bankrolling its popularization.)

As money played an ever greater role in American politics, perceptions of corruption grew. If you combine that with a general skepticism about Washington; a political movement focused on making the government the villain; a special focus of attacks on a part of the government that was, at least in theory, beyond the reach of voters; growing polarization; growing inequality; and an acute sense that DC was not working for all the people equally, then the poll numbers about plummeting trust in our institutions make sense. (The effort by the party that was most associated with the interests of the top one percent to redirect the anger of the people away from their super-empowered benefactors to the bureaucracy also makes perfect sense.)

But there is a problem with all of this.

The view I have developed over nearly forty years of working in and around Washington, despite my acute familiarity with the flaws of our system, is very much at odds with the negativity you read in op-ed columns, or hear from certain politicians in their stump speeches.

I warn you in advance. Some people may find this point, which happens to be the central thrust of this book, triggering. But take a deep breath and hear me out. Not only are there good people in Washington, but most of the people who work in the US government are actually fundamentally good, well intentioned, and trying to make a positive difference for America.

Good People Doing Good Work

To begin with, greater Washington, DC, by definition as home to the federal government, the largest organization in the world, has a higher percentage of residents who have devoted their lives to public service than anywhere else in the world. Again, I am not excusing the behavior of the corrupt and the odious in the system. Instead, I am suggesting that the character of the community in which the business of our nation takes place, of the government, and of the people within it is quite different from that which current conventional wisdom suggests.

My perspective is, of course, shaped in part by my own experience.

Growing up, my exposure to the world of the US government was limited to lively dinner table conversations in our suburban New Jersey home. I think we made one trip to DC when I was a kid. My parents took us to the Capitol, to the office of a senator from New Jersey, to the FBI building, and to the US Mint. We had dinner in a smoky Washington steak house called Blackie's and I remember spending the entire night, age ten or so, huddled over the tickertape machine by the front entrance, amazed there was a device that could reveal news as it happened.

Other than the confident predictions of a long-gone aunt whom I believed would surely be America's first Jewish president, that was the totality of my exposure to the nation's capital, or what went on there, until I began to look for a job following a brief, undistinguished stint at the Columbia University Graduate School of Journalism.

On the job board in that school's career placement office was an index card indicating that a young congressman from Brooklyn named Stephen J. Solarz was looking for a press secretary. While I had no experience, the Columbia credential was apparently a good one. I had founded and run the student television station while I was an undergraduate, and

I had co-written a slim textbook on the European community (admittedly, my co-author was my mother). Due to all these factors—and perhaps also a result of the fact that I had removed the job card from the board and taken it with me so there would be no one else who could apply for the position—I got the job. My first in the US government, my first in the world of Washington, DC, and politics.

From my first days in that very first job, I was struck by the qualities of people in Washington you do not much hear or read about. Virtually everyone in the office in which I worked was really deeply interested in public policy, in making life better for average people. But it was more than that. The congressman for whom I worked, Steve Solarz, was deeply interested in foreign policy and, as it turned out, I was too. He took pains to teach me a great deal. I learned by writing op-eds and bits of speeches for him, and he generously played the role of professor in correcting and reshaping and improving my work.

The chief of staff in his office was a man named Michael Lewan. Mike was generous with his time and a mentor to the generally young staff (and to be fair, he was not much older than most of us). My direct boss was a woman named Mary Jane Burt. I remember that when I would go to Washington to visit the DC office, she would let me sleep on her couch; and one or two times I also was invited to stay with the Solarz family. There was a sense of welcoming and teamwork that, to be honest, I have felt in many if not all of my Washington jobs.

Most of the time, to my chagrin, my work was not on Capitol Hill, which I found very glamorous, but instead was in the Brooklyn field office of the congressman. There, most of the operation was devoted to constituent service. We sat in one big room at two rows of desks, so I could hear all the calls. One day, at the desk immediately behind mine, one of the staff, a much older guy, answered the phone and I heard him say, very seriously, "Yes, ma'am. Yes, ma'am. Now, now, ma'am, please calm down and tell me what is wrong." And there was silence and periodically he would offer a sound of listening and taking it in: "Mmm-hmmm. Mmm-hmmm. Yes, ma'am."

After about ten minutes of listening, he said: "Well, you know, ma'am, I really think this is a police matter. If you like, I can connect you to the precinct." He was comforting in his tone. Soon after, he hung up. I asked what the call was about and he said that it was an old woman who sometimes called. She was mostly lonely and wanted someone to talk to. This time the call was about a plate of cream cheese that had gone missing from her refrigerator. I looked at him and he offered a small smile. But it was compassionate. He was not making fun of her. He was just offering her a willing ear when she needed one.

That does not sound very dramatic, I know. But there was an aspect to that moment and that call that cut to the essence of much of what I saw at many different levels during the past four decades, including the last thirty years of almost constant involvement in Washington at a fairly high level.

Time and time again during my years in Washington, I have been struck by the quality of the people with whom I worked. Whether they were top officials—presidents and cabinet members—or young bureaucrats or military officers or diplomats just starting out, they were all actually making the choice to serve their country. Many could have made much more money had they chosen a different career path.

In my particular field of work, which thanks in large part to the inspiration and guidance of Steve Solarz became international relations and national security, there was for most of my time in Washington a real effort to set aside partisan differences. Among the policy community with whom I dealt, most of the people I worked with were genuinely interested in advancing national interests.

Yes, Washington has its share of operators and sleazeballs. But in my nearly four decades of dealing with the place, they were in the minority. Yes, many in Washington were a bit too risk averse, a bit too conformist, too afraid to rock the boat—but there were exceptions to these rules as well. The place is a little too Brooks Brothers and Ann Taylor for my taste. But there was from almost everyone I encountered in and around the US government almost all the time an essential quality that I have come to value a great deal. It is a commitment to service. Periodically it is obscured by ambition or ideological factors. But time and time again, in far more cases than otherwise, watch carefully enough and you will see it is there. What is more, it endures no matter which way the political winds are blowing.

We are fortunate that it does. Because if you want to build a resilient system, if you want to be sure that an organization, no matter how large or small, can survive whatever fate may have in store for it—although having clear organizing principles, rules, and institutional structure matters—in the end your strength, your ability to adapt, your ability to identify and correct errors, and your ability to grow all depend first and foremost on people, the human factor.

When I researched my first book on how Washington works at the top, *Running the World: The Inside Story of the National Security Council and the Architects of American Power*, my biggest takeaway was that while most analysts, academics, and commentators focused on "the three *P*s"—politics, process, and policy—the crucial difference between successful and unsuccessful administrations was a fourth *P*—people. In the same way, it is the people who occupy the more than one million positions in the US government that ensure the American experiment survives from administration to administration, no matter who passes through the revolving door at the top.

The story of those people is often mundane. Many of them, even those at very senior levels of government, operate far from the public eye, doing work that might seem to people in the outside world arcane or even tedious. But it must be done in order to make the government work. And, periodically, events conspire to remind us how important that work is.

Heroes and Villains

Among the times that the value of official Washington becomes most clear is when our system of government is tested. Sometimes those tests come from without, from natural disasters or wars, civil unrest, or pandemics. Ironically, as we have recently learned, another time that we are reminded about what is best and most valuable within our system is when our government is abused or mismanaged or attacked from within.

It is at those moments, a period like we lived through during the eventful, often deeply disturbing years of the Trump administration, when we discover that far from being unaccountable, officials within our government reveal how seriously they take the idea that they serve the American people, how seriously they take their oath to the Constitution and the concept of duty. In so doing, through their actions they reveal a far different side to Washington than that which is typically offered up on the news, or snarked about on Twitter. It is not just a story that happens to conform more closely with my own personal experience of many years in Washington. It also offers insights into how our government really works, which is far different from what is written about in textbooks or taught in university classrooms.

Anyone who watched the January 6 Committee hearings or who followed their progress knows that there were many people in the Trump Administration who, though loyal to Trump at one time, ultimately came to recognize the threat posed by Trump. Some questioned the president's actions from within. Some challenged them publicly as they happened by resigning. Some ultimately helped make the case against Trump for the committee by cooperating with investigators and telling the truth. Often taking a stand took a toll on their careers. Many faced—as did Trump's own Vice President on January 6—grave threats to their lives from the extremists who formed the core of former president Trump's base.

It became clear that for many, Trump's effort to steal the 2020 election was too outrageous for these public servants to endure. One by one, we listened as they bore witness. Some, like former acting attorney general Jeffrey Rosen; acting deputy attorney general Richard Donoghue; former White House counsel Pat Cipollone; Greg Jacob, top aide to Vice President Pence; and Cassidy Hutchinson, former aide to Trump chief of staff Mark Meadows were spotlighted by the committee. Others testified behind closed doors. But it cannot be denied that the strongest case against Trump and one of the greatest obstacles to any future political plans he may have, ultimately came from people within the administration. Indeed, it also must be acknowledged that the two Republicans who broke with their colleagues to participate on the committee, Representative Liz

Cheney and Representative Adam Kinzinger, played an absolutely central role in ensuring that the crimes of the former president and those closest to him were revealed and that the process by which that was done was, in fact, bipartisan.

However you may assess the actions of these individuals at other points during their service to the Trump Administration, it cannot be denied that at a moment when former president Trump tried to claim an office to which he was no longer entitled, we were fortunate to have in and around our government people who in different ways stood up to protect our institutions and values.

That is both a remarkable thing and an encouraging one. But, vast as the Trump conspiracy was and as extensive as the efforts to stop him and call him out may have been, the story told by the January 6 Committee is just the tip of the iceberg. Similar stories of resistance occurred throughout the government and protected us from outcomes at home and around the world that were even more dire than what we actually experienced during the Trump years.

I have tried to tell some of those stories here in this book, stories of how an informal alliance of women and men working in agencies across the US government, some at the highest level, some several levels down, some well known, some obscure, some Republicans, some Democrats, some Independents, worked together to keep a dangerous, unhinged, ill-prepared president and his closest allies from doing irreparable damage to the United States, its people, our allies, and to the planet as a whole.

It is a story of preventing wars, crimes, needless deaths, and the undermining of US democracy.

It is not a simple story. Many very disturbing things happened along the way. And sometimes the people who did not do enough to stop one set of bad events from unfolding—or even contributed to deeply misguided or dangerous policies or actions—later stepped up and played a vital role to ensure even worse things did not subsequently happen.

As a result, it is a story of heroes and villains in which sometimes those who served the country in important ways let the country down in other ways. Each reader can make their own judgment about the overall quality of the service or the character of those whose stories are told here. But it should also be clear that sometimes what the news presents as black and white while it is happening is actually something else, and that partisanship is a distortionary lens through which to view complex issues and events. And it should also be clear that as bad as much of what occurred during the Trump years was, it could have been much, much worse.

In fact, I think in the end this book will reveal that during a period in which the threat to our democracy was greater than at any time since the Civil War, time after time it turns out it was those who some condemned as members of the (non-existent) deep state that actually helped save the country . . . or at least did their best to protect it. It was their commitment to the Constitution and character that defeated, slowed, or diluted many of the most insidious and dangerous ideas of President Donald Trump and his small inner circle of loyalists.

It should be noted that some of those whose stories are featured in this book were actually political appointees, hand selected by the Trump administration. These included members of the cabinet, the sub-cabinet, and senior officials who despite being committed Republicans placed the interests of the country first—even when it triggered the Twitter bombs, behind-closed-door tantrums, and retaliation from Trump and the sharpshooters around him.

While my view of Washington, forty years after I first got that job with Steve Solarz, may not jibe with the partisan tropes or lazy Hollywood depictions, one of the reasons I am writing this book is because those views are not only deeply wrong, but they have been weaponized to attack the vital institutions of our government. Weakening those institutions is good news for billionaires and big companies who would like to set their own rules for doing business. And, as we have seen more recently, it serves the interests of wannabe autocrats who would like to gut the very idea of democracy. Also, as we saw during the Trump administration, framing career officials or others who have devoted much of their lives to government as part of some shadowy, untrustworthy secret club made it easier to justify firing them and replacing them with those who placed loyalty to the president ahead of loyalty to the Constitution or the country.

Finally, by vilifying the so-called deep state we undercut the vital impulse toward public service that is essential in any society; we make it harder for good people to do their jobs; and we make it easier for bad people to get away with abuse and even criminal activity.

That was the objective of former president Trump and his hardcore acolytes, as the more than one hundred interviews I did for this book underscored. While many of those closest to the president did not understand much about how the government worked when they took office, they gradually grew to understand the nature of most of those public servants, the seriousness with which they took their obligation to the public and the institutions in which they served. Further, as time went by Trump and his inner circle started to purge the deep state officials and even a considerable number of senior Trump appointees, not simply on abstract grounds of loyalty but because many of them were actively and effectively seeking to resist the president's most dangerous, irrational, or corrupt impulses.

Fortunately for all of us—at least during the four years of Trump's presidency—the good people within our system regularly rebuffed and defeated the efforts of those who attacked them and the values for which they stood. When other checks and balances failed, when the Congress chose not to undertake supervision as it should or the president thumbed his nose at that oversight without being held to account, or when leaders in the Justice Department neutered many of the legal avenues by which the president's abuses might be curbed, it was the character of the people within the system that saved the country.

Like the voters who in 2018 and 2020 rejected the lies and agenda of the Trump administration, America's public servants stepped up and, sometimes far from the public eye, served as the conscience of the government. From racist bans on immigration to the United States to reckless rejection of science in the face of a pandemic, from the reckless use of military force to the undermining of our elections, dangerous plans were stopped by good people doing their jobs.

William Taylor, a former ambassador to Ukraine, a distinguished diplomat, and a former soldier who was one of those whose voices were first heard by many during impeachment hearings against the president, viewed the United States as having during this period two governments. There was what he called the "regular channel"—the one that had operated as intended under the laws, traditions, and precedents that had guided past administrations. And then there was the "irregular channel"—in the case of the Ukraine scandal and the Rudy Giuliani demi-monde. Others with whom I spoke, including several former Trump cabinet officials, regularly referred to the Trump inner circle as the "crazies" or the "true-believers." In virtually every instance in which I discussed this division within the government, there was the sense that Trump, his family, and his closest advisors did not trust the world of official Washington.

The president himself, in the words of one former cabinet official, was "pathological" about the issue of loyalty to him and in his resentment of those (including, ultimately, many of "his generals") once trusted protectors like Attorney Generals Sessions and Barr, and even his vice president, whom he saw as having committed the ultimate sin of betraying him in order instead to serve the country. From James Comey to Ambassador Marie Yovanovitch to more than one of Trump's chiefs of staff, many paid for doing their duty and were summarily dismissed, their careers broken.

Fortunately, the antipathy of the president and the firings and the Twitter rants and the toxic environment did not deter hundreds and hundreds of high-level officials from doing their jobs. Some found what former Homeland Security secretary Kirstjen Nielsen and members of her team characterized as "workarounds" in which they could collaborate with others who were committed to honoring the law while also respecting the authority and role of the presidency. These might include informal meetings of cabinet members, as was the case when a team worked to ensure the security of the 2020 elections. Or the advisors from the White House, State Department, and Defense Department who dealt with Russia-related issues; they knew that Trump would react "irrationally" on these questions and, wherever possible, sought to bypass him.

In every case with which I have become familiar in the course of reporting for this book, these approaches were legal and appropriate (in my estimation; I'm not a lawyer). Indeed, these officials were doing what their jobs as well as their values required. In a number of cases, doing what their president wanted would have been disastrous or criminal or both.

As a historian of how the White House works, I have tried to scrupulously present the stories of these actors in their own words. From time to time, to ensure context was clear and to give as much of a first-person feel as possible to the events being described, I have used somewhat longer, uninterrupted quotations. In some instances, where requested, I have protected the identities of those with whom I spoke because they feared recriminations. Indeed, many with whom I spoke had gone public with their criticisms of the Trump administration and experienced harassment and even death threats simply for doing their jobs as they believed they should be done.

The issues discussed remain contentious, and the ferocity of partisan exchanges these days is one of those things that leads people to think that all of Washington is broken. Fortunately, many of those with whom I spoke have put their comments on the record because they felt the story of what worked when much else in the government was under attack or failing was worth telling.

I should note that several of those with whom I spoke objected to the title of the book, *American Resistance*. They felt they were not resisting but instead were actually simply carrying out the essence of what their jobs required. In fact, they prided themselves on their loyalty and their steadfastness. It was not they who had deviated. In their view, they were just doing their jobs, and their actions could only be seen as resistant because some at the top, beginning with the man in the Oval Office, were abusing their power, breaking the law, and actually attacking the institutions they were supposed to be leading and the values and laws they were supposed to be defending.

In Their Own Words

Others were uncomfortable being characterized as part of the deep state. Some saw the term as derogatory. Others felt its use would play into the hands of the conspiracy theorists who popularized the term during the Trump years.

When the term "deep state" became popular in 2017, some friends and I started a podcast called *Deep State Radio*. Almost seven hundred episodes later, we are now a regular meeting place for current and former government officials, journalists, and experts to discuss national security, foreign policy, and broader public policy and political issues. We have, as of this writing, been downloaded over 11 million times. And in each and every episode, one thing we have been doing is trying to reveal the deep state conspiracy theories for the dangerous, silly, and misguided nonsense they are. The best way to do this, we felt, was to allow people who came from within the system to reveal themselves, their motives, their thoughts, and thereby the truth about who they were.

That approach is precisely the one I seek to follow in this book. The goal is to let members of the so-called deep state speak for themselves and in so doing reveal the essential role they played, why they were so valuable, and why the conspiracy theories denigrating them are so dangerous. By telling as much of the story as possible in their own words, it also allows us to cut through the spin and the disinformation and the distortionary bubbles of modern media "echo-systems." We need these people. We should be grateful for them, and it is certainly my hope that this modest volume helps in some small way to make that case.

The book begins with a look at when officials involved in the Trump administration realized it would be different from any past government experience virtually all of them had. Then, a handful of key participants share their perspectives on how they and their colleagues helped defuse bad policy ideas and periodically averted or undid disastrous decisions, among them the effort to ban Muslim entry into the United States; Trump's conflicts with "his generals" and the military; the Russia-Ukraine case that led to Trump's impeachment; the COVID crisis; and the elections and January 6 uprising. Along the way, we can see how people balanced their oaths to the Constitution and working within the hierarchy of the US government. Each case allows us to draw certain lessons and offer some ideas about what might come next.

There is an old saying that "an institution is just the lengthened shadow of one person." That may be true in some companies. It is the objective in autocracies. It must not be true in a democracy or a government of laws. Instead, the greatness of our institutions lies in the quality of the characters of the many people working within them because they, in the end, are the ones who determine the values by which we are governed, who make the millions of daily choices that are crucial elements of governance. And, of course, in a democracy the ones who are truly in charge, whose values really should matter most, are the members of the electorate, the people. In some respects, in a well-functioning democracy elected officials are at the bottom of the totem poll, reporting up to the citizenry at large.

While the media tend to want to focus on individuals because doing so makes for simpler, more easily digested narratives, the truth is more complex and more collective. Government is a collaboration—between and among those within the government and those who remain, so far, in charge in our democracy, the voters.

Our system is not perfect, but there is a grace and resilience and wisdom within it that comes from the fact that so many people participate in the business of making our government work. Further, cognizant though we may be of the inevitable flaws within our system and all bureaucracies, we should also be aware that we have long been fortunate to have had so many good men and women devote themselves to serving the public. There are many examples around the world of societies and systems that are not so lucky, including, tellingly, some of those that supported, were supported by, and emulated by President Trump, his political allies, and the MAGA (Make America Great Again) movement. Vladimir Putin's Russia comes to mind.

While these ideas may sound Pollyanna-ish to some, recent experience shows that in fact they are the opposite. It is the character of the majority who have served in our government that has been our last bulwark of defense against those who are corrupt, malevolent, or misguided. For the past forty years, growing inequality in American society has enabled the few to gain ever more influence within our government, which in turn has enabled them to gain ever greater rewards, compounding the economic and political inequalities in our society again and again.

As noted earlier, big corporations and rich activists have sought to tilt the playing field ever further and more permanently in their direction, both by supporting policies that attack government and its ability to tax and regulate and enforce the law, and by rewiring the political system so their

supporters can gain and maintain power. This has in turn contributed to the weakening of vital checks and balances within
our system. They built up the wealth of a few and a handful
of chosen, politically aggressive industries—from the defense
sector to Big Pharma, Big Oil to tech and Wall Street. It is
easy to understand why the poet and songwriter Leonard Cohen, quoted at the outset of this introduction, concluded: "The
killers are in control."

Furthermore, as we have seen, a president whose party
controls the Senate and the Department of Justice and the
courts can effectively operate above and beyond the reach of
the law. And, as we have also seen, such a president and his
supporters have it within their reach to eviscerate our democracy and for all intents and purposes end it. Indeed, it is undeniable that for some—supporters of the Big Lie, supporters of
former president Trump—that still remains their goal.

What they discovered however was that while in government, even when the Congress and the Department of Justice
and the courts were compliant with their wishes, there remained throughout the government brave souls willing to risk
their careers to uphold a Constitution that the president and
his supporters saw only as a series of suggestions from which
they could opt out at will. It so frustrated Trump and his allies that they made it their explicit goal to identify and root
out these patriots within our system. They made considerable
progress in this regard, filling crucial positions in the Department of Defense, the State Department, the Department of
Homeland Security, and the Intelligence Community with
loyalist apparatchiks. But they could not replace everyone or
undermine the bedrock sense of duty that is the foundation of
public service.

On issue after issue the plans of the wreckers were thwarted.

Whatever we call those who succeeded on behalf of the American people—the "deep state" or the "resistance" or just public officials doing their duty—we owe them not just a debt of gratitude. We owe them both an appreciation for the role they played and an ongoing, resolute commitment to preserving their ability and that of those like them to continue to serve the Constitution rather than the whims of any one man or woman or political faction.

You do not have to love or admire their politics or every aspect of their careers to be grateful that when it mattered they acted to defend the interests of the country. Indeed, some of these people will no doubt be criticized for seeking to launder their reputations by telling their behind-the-scenes stories now. You can make your own judgments about whether they are doing that. What I have tried to do is to verify that their stories are accurate and to recount instances in which, in my view, they did make a difference for the better. That said, the roles played by others whose stories are told here are indisputably admirable, some even heroic, because they not only served their country but they also did so at great personal and professional risk.

In other words, the stories told in this book do not just depict Washington during a few dark and challenging years in our history. They also capture much of the spirit of service that has helped this country endure other such chapters in the past—and will be essential if we are to face the threats and tap the potential the future will certainly bring.

David Rothkopf
New York City, Spring 2022

CHAPTER ONE

Walking into a Blast Furnace

Never let yourself be persuaded that any one Great
Man, any one leader, is necessary to the salvation of
America. When America consists of one leader and
158 million followers, it will no longer be America.

—**DWIGHT D. EISENHOWER**

E VEN MANY OF those who would play important roles in
Donald Trump's administration knew from very early on
that it would not be like others in American history. And
not in a good way. But many who signed on did so because they
thought the job would change the man or that the great apparatus of Washington would act as a constraint on his worst impulses. Some even held out hope that he would grow into the job.

But that was in the very beginning. Soon what hopes there
were began to fade.

Others, including myself, felt Donald Trump's victory
would be a catastrophe. Before the election, I joined with

my colleagues at *Foreign Policy* to publish the magazine's first editorial in its fifty-year history to ever take sides in a presidential election. On behalf of our editorial team, I wrote that we felt it necessary to make "clear the great magnitude of the threat that a Donald Trump presidency would pose to the United States. The dangers Trump presents as president stretch beyond the United States to the international economy, to global security, to America's allies, as well as to countless innocents everywhere who would be the victims of his inexperience, his perverse policy views, and the profound unsuitability of his temperament for the office he seeks." I cited the dangers of his closeness to Vladimir Putin, his cronies' ties to Russia, his forgiveness of Russia's invasion of Crimea, his reckless attitude toward nuclear weapons, and his insults to our neighbors and allies. We identified as particular problems his vilification of Muslims, his denial of science, his narcissism, his denigration of the US military, and his lack of respect for the rule of law. Concluding our assessment, we argued that he would "put at risk our way of life, our freedoms and our alliances," and that he was "a destabilizing force that would undercut American leadership instantly and for generations to come."

All that was clear before the election. What was not clear, even to members of his inner circle (as we later would learn), was that he would be elected, or how quickly he would start to fulfill our most dire expectations.

A Surreal Walk through a Stunned City

By eight o'clock on the night of November 8, 2016, the Comedy Cellar on west Third Street in Manhattan was rocking.

It was packed. More than two hundred New Yorkers were crowded into booths and around tables drinking, celebrating, and laughing at every joke the comedians were serving up.

It was an election-night party hosted by our magazine. The idea behind the party was to shake off a little of *Foreign Policy*'s traditional sobriety with an unorthodox take on the breaking news of the election that had pitted Hillary Clinton against Donald Trump. Seasoned analysts, many who were contributors to the magazine and who appeared on its weekly podcast, offered their take on unfolding events and updates, and every so often comedians did the same.

It was raucous. Early in the evening, the infamous *New York Times* "needle," which pointed which way the election seemed to be heading, had been showing an 85 percent likelihood that Hillary Clinton would win. A show of hands revealed the crowd was about 90 percent pro-Clinton (close to her actual results in Manhattan).

But it was also clear as the first results started coming in that the election might be closer than predicted. By half past eight, jokes about finally having the first woman president in US history were met with nervous laughter. People stopped watching the stage. They weren't even watching the big-screen TVs all around the room. They were looking at their phones. They were staring at the *New York Times* needle, trying to will it to stay in pro-Clinton territory.

But the collective psychic push they and millions of others were directing at the needle did not work. Around nine, it tipped in Trump's direction. The *New York Times* was predicting that Donald Trump, a man universally loathed and denigrated by anyone who had followed his career, the man *Spy* magazine regularly referred to as a "short-fingered vulgarian," the reality TV host, Atlantic City huckster, the cheesiest public figure in America, very likely was going to be the next president of the United States.

Soon the room was silent. A woman wearing a trench coat, which she was clutching tightly around her, murmured, "I need to . . . throw . . . up." The stress had gotten to her. The comedians, not feeling any positive feedback in the room, were turning hostile. Outside, the city was post-apocalyptic. Empty streets. Few cars. People walked blocks without seeing anyone else. It was surreal.

Around two-thirty in the morning, it was announced that Hillary Clinton, whose victory I had been predicting with great confidence for weeks, often on television or radio shows, had conceded to Trump. Her public concession speech did not come until the next morning. Friends of mine who had worked closely with the former secretary of state sat in rows in front of her, some weeping. Jake Sullivan, her top policy advisor, who would later become national security advisor to President Joe Biden and who had been a friend for a long time, seemed particularly obliterated. It was hard to watch.

Later we would learn that in the Trump camp expectations of victory had been low throughout Election Day. One Trump advisor with whom I spoke said: "I don't think anyone of us expected him to win. I don't think he expected to win. I know I did not believe it was happening, even as the networks announced it. It was like being in a dream, an out-of-body experience."

Some accounts of the night suggested Trump simply refused to acknowledge victory because he was superstitious. According to one ABC News account, daughter-in-law Lara Trump reported: "Everybody kept coming up and saying, 'We think we have Pennsylvania. We have it. You're going to win, you're going to be the next president,' and he said, 'I don't want to know until it's real, until someone has made it official.'"

Of course, what the people who silently filed out of the Comedy Cellar that night knew, which many who voted for Trump, or were even in the room celebrating with him on election night did not, was how utterly unprepared Donald Trump was to be president and how profoundly ill-suited he was to the demands of the job. It was a matter of public record, of course. The man who won with a minority of the popular vote, but an edge in the Electoral College, was the only person ever elected president of the United States who did not have a single minute of public service experience. Every other elected president in US history had served in public office or the military. Trump did not have a clue as to how the government worked. Nor, as it turned out, did he really care to learn. "He was the president," said one member of his cabinet. "He assumed we would learn how to work as he wanted and that, rather than established procedures or even laws and regulations, was all that mattered."

"It Was a Mess"

Anyone who had assumed Trump would be able to hire people who could guide him (or more importantly that he would listen to) soon got the first warning this was unlikely to happen. Within days of being elected, Trump scrapped his transition team led by former New Jersey governor Chris Christie and began as chaotic, fractious, and incompetent a transition process as anyone had ever seen. Josh Bolten, former chief of staff to George W. Bush and a man with considerable transition experience, said: "It was a mess. It looked like a mess

from the outside, and based on the conversations I had with
people who were speaking to the team, interviewing for jobs,
it looked like a mess from the inside, too."

In fact, from the start Trump had been resistant to the
idea of even having a transition committee. When he was informed it was the law, he submitted to the idea and to Christie's suggestion of himself as its chief. But he saw the process
as intrusive and unnecessary. He felt that when the time came,
he and a small group of advisors could pick a cabinet and handle any questions that came up. That, after all, was the way
he had run his company. The fact that the US government
has 2 million employees and is mind-bogglingly complex, or
that there were thousands of political appointments his team
would be expected to make, twelve hundred of which would
require Senate confirmation, did not seem to have crossed his
mind.

As Michael Lewis observed in his book *The Fifth Risk*,
Trump was leery of the costs of such a committee. Perhaps
it was because he did not think he would really win. Perhaps
it was because he saw every dollar raised for his campaign as
his own money, and he did not wish to siphon off a cash flow
that was ending up in his own pocket. Before the election
was decided, and while Trump still thought his chances of
winning were slight, he erupted more than once when told of
the costs of the transition committee, or of Christie's fund-
raising to underwrite it. Lewis described how Trump lashed
out and fired Christie for "stealing his money." When the federal law requiring the campaign to have such a committee
was described to Trump by Christie and the CEO of Trump's
campaign, Stephen Bannon, his response, according to Lewis,
was: "Fuck the law, I don't give a fuck about the law. I want
my fucking money."

It was a phrase so emblematic of the presidency to come that it should be considered for the inscription over the entrance to the Trump presidential library, should one ever be built.

Trump had demanded the transition be "shut down." Christie and Bannon walked Trump back on this, thanks to quick thinking by Bannon. He played to Trump's ego and suggested shutting down the transition committee would be interpreted as a sign he thought he was going to lose. But the incident revealed volumes about Trump's volatility and his complete resistance to the necessary steps involved in governing the country.

Planning was something he generally looked down upon. A Politico story by Nancy Cook quoted one member of Trump's transition team reflecting on the contrast in 2016 with what happened in 2020: "Trump famously thinks preparation is for losers, and the Biden team appears to be the opposite. Trump never wanted to prepare for a meeting because he thought he could wing it, and that you only have to prepare if you are not naturally good or can't think on your feet."

Another problem that cropped up during the 2016 transition process, and that would haunt the administration, was the division between government professionals trying to do their jobs and Trump's inner circle. That inner circle included his children, his son-in-law Jared Kushner, Steve Bannon, and a tight group who worked out of his New York office. They created a kind of analog for the way he ran his family-owned real estate business, catering to his needs and isolating him from the world. This group included Hope Hicks, John McEntee, Stephen Miller, and Kellyanne Conway. They would all go on to hold key White House posts.

Christie's team soldiered on doing what transitions typically require, identifying potential hires and potential policy priorities and preparing background materials on them. Christie would then have to run the results by Kushner and the Trump offspring for their approval. They would ask superficial questions, but dug deep on no one and no thing.

Christie, when he was attorney general in New Jersey, had prosecuted Kushner's father and ultimately got him sent to jail. He also uncovered Kushner senior's unsavory business practices, including hiring a hooker to sleep with his son-in-law in order to have leverage over him on business matters. Although Kushner and Christie held a kind of truce during the last months of the campaign, their mutual loathing was hidden from no one in their orbit.

A Transition in Spite of Itself

As a consequence, when Christie was fired as transition director just days after the election, he was unsurprised to hear from Bannon that it was Kushner who had pushed him out. But the inner circle did not just push out Christie. Ultimately, they jettisoned most of the transition team and took on the job of picking cabinet secretaries themselves. It was an idea even Bannon found troubling. He was the one who had to go to the transition offices and fire everyone. According to Lewis, Bannon would later say: "I was fucking nervous as shit. I go, 'Holy fuck, this guy [Trump] doesn't know anything. And he doesn't give a shit.'"

Russell Berman, in the *Atlantic* magazine, explained how Trump adopted the theatrics of good government when in fact the decision-making process was falling apart. The president-elect "made a show of naming members of his cabinet in rapid succession, giving the impression that his transition was proceeding speedily. But the slew of nominations obscured an important detail: Trump's team had done little or no vetting of those appointees before or immediately after the election."

Routinely, candidates for positions in this next administration were not required to provide the background-check information normally expected of prospective federal government employees: the kind that would satisfy the FBI and weather financial scrutiny. The transition prescreening, which could take months, had not begun until November or even December, barely a month before Trump was due to take office.

Many of the executives picked by Trump were very rich and had complex financial portfolios, which made vetting them difficult. The result of this reckless process was that some of those who were nominated had challenging confirmation processes. Wilbur Ross, who would become commerce secretary, would have questions lingering over his financial dealings throughout the Trump presidency. Andrew Puzder, nominated for labor secretary, ultimately had to withdraw from consideration because of allegations of spousal abuse, allegations of mistreating his employees at the restaurant chain he ran, and for having a housekeeper for whom he did not properly pay taxes. In a normal transition process, any one of these problems would have been flagged, possibly ensuring the individual involved was not nominated.

Trump preferred to operate from his gut. He told his team one of his criteria was finding people who "looked the part." He wanted "brand name" nominees like former Exxon Mobil CEO Rex Tillerson, whom he named his top diplomat; or Senator Jeff Sessions, whom he named attorney general; or his "generals." These were former top military officials like General James Mattis, named for secretary of defense;

General John Kelly, named for secretary of homeland security; and General Michael Flynn, named for national security
advisor.

Flynn is a conspicuous example of how awry the process
went, and what a bad judge of character Trump was. (See
also former campaign chairman and convicted felon Paul
Manafort on that front.) The Christie transition team had not
included Flynn among their nominees for the National Security Council (NSC) job. One of the team told me that "everyone we spoke to warned us he was a loose cannon. One guy
told me he thought he was unstable. After all, he had been
fired by Barack Obama. But Trump, apparently, saw that as a
qualification."

The Christie transition team's nominations were reviewed
by a group that included Trump's daughter Ivanka and Flynn
himself. During the "review" Ivanka apparently asked Flynn
which job he wanted, and the rest is history. He lasted twenty-
four days as national security advisor. In 2017, he pleaded
guilty to lying to the FBI about his contacts with Russia's
ambassador Sergey Kislyak. Trump would later pardon Flynn
but by that time, November 2020, Flynn was leading an effort among the most extreme of Trump's supporters to use the
military to seize voting machines and, ultimately, try to reverse the outcome of the 2020 presidential election, a contest
Trump lost by 8 million votes.

The entire period from the transition to when Trump took
the oath of office on January 20, 2017, was in the eyes of one
member of the transition team with whom I spoke: "A clusterfuck. I had served before. I knew Washington. I had never
seen anything like this. There were leaks. There was bitter
infighting between the Trump inner circle and we who were
considered hired hands."

"I don't think they ever trusted us fully, even when some of us, as I did, ended up in the administration," one former senior official admitted. "And sometimes we would get together after work and we would talk about what we were seeing, and decide who we could reach out to up the chain who might listen to why the process would only lead to problems in the long run. But I can tell you, while sometimes some folks sounded reasonable—Ivanka, for example, was considered more reasonable than the others—nothing changed. Because all of this was driven by one person, by Trump."

When the Penny Dropped

I asked this official why he stayed, why he didn't just avoid the "clusterfuck" as soon as it was obvious. His answer was one I heard often. He said: "Because I thought I could make a difference. Because, honestly, when I looked at what was going on around me, I thought I was needed. I'm not saying I am somehow special. I just felt that given how little most of the people at the top knew about how the government works, we needed some professionals."

Elaine McCusker, who would later serve as deputy under secretary of defense (comptroller) for Trump, and who later put her career at risk by flagging Trump's illegal stoppage of congressionally mandated aid payments to Ukraine, observed: "I think the process the Trump administration went through to select and vet its political appointees was probably a bit different from other transitions, because they didn't have the kind of government experience to quickly identify and hire experts." McCusker added that there was "not a good communication process. They were kind of learning as they went along."

Christopher Ford, who would serve in the Trump administration as assistant secretary of state for arms control and international security, described his experience: "I, as probably most people, was surprised by how things actually went on election night in '16. I had been doing some internal policy papers on foreign affairs and national security issues for the pre-election Republican Party operation, but there was little expectation that this would be anything other than a sort of academic exercise. But a few days after Trump was elected, I got a call saying, 'Hey, you know, would you like to join the transition team?' so that was sort of my first entrée into the Trump world. I got the impression at the time that they really hadn't been expecting to win, and so they were well behind the curve in setting up what you would have considered to be a proper fully staffed and well-organized transition apparatus. It seemed like a pretty fly-by-the-seat-of-your-pants effort, with a lot of folks who hadn't done this kind of thing before, and with a 'Holy shit, we just found out we won, what do we do now?' kind of vibe. Lots of on the job learning there."

For many members of the Trump administration, as in Ford's case, the transition was the moment "the penny dropped," to use a phrase I heard several times. For others, that came early in the administration. Those who had served before recognized that the Trump administration would be unlike any other that they had seen, perhaps unlike any in American history. But even those who had not previously served in senior executive branch jobs felt like something was off.

Almost all of them told me they felt these problems were "growing pains." Certainly in US history there have been plenty of examples of administrations struggling with a learning curve, of nominations not getting confirmed, of senior officials having to resign fairly early in the administration. In the Clinton administration (in which I served) that was the case. In that administration there was also the tension between Clinton insiders, many of whom hailed from Arkansas or the schools attended by the Clintons, and Washington professionals. Identifying someone as being from Little Rock was both an acknowledgment they were an insider and, for some, a term of derision. (Similarly, so was the acronym FOB for "friend of Bill.")

The learning curve ultimately cost Clinton's kindergarten friend Mack McLarty, who became White House chief of staff, his job within eighteen months, even though McLarty was in no way akin to the unqualified Trump inner circle. He was and is a very successful businessman, a former member of the Arkansas House of Representatives, and a former Democratic Party chair in Arkansas. He is also a very good and decent man. But running the White House is one of the hardest jobs on earth, and it is made much harder when the president does not have much Washington experience.

Even though George W. Bush was similarly from "outside DC," because his father had served as president only eight years prior to his taking office, his team was full of experienced professionals, most notably Dick Cheney, a former defense secretary who tasked with finding a vice president, ended up finding himself. So experience alone isn't necessarily a virtue. Bush's team during their first term made some absolutely catastrophic decisions (like going to war in Iraq). But Bush grew in office and was considerably more successful during his second term as a consequence.

Barack Obama was also a relative newcomer to Washington. He was surrounded by an inner circle from his Senate office and his Chicago years, which led to similar problems.

Fortunately, he also had the help of a number of former top Clinton officials. He also took office in the midst of a once-in-a-generation economic crisis, and his new team was forced into very close coordination with his predecessors during the Bush-Obama transition. That handover is widely considered more successful than many.

Some of Trump's team was drawn from the Bush administration. Some were career military. Some came from Capitol Hill. All of them had easier adjustments and more experience to draw on than those who came from the corporate world. Trump had sold himself as a problem solver from the business world and valued people with similar experience. But running a business is in no way like running a big government agency, a fact they were all to discover, to their chagrin, as early as the first months of the administration.

What unites the experiences of all those who served in the Trump administration, however, is that at the moment "the penny dropped" for them, they were not only taken aback, but also were given a glimpse into the administration's essential nature. Sometimes they did not immediately understand what they were witnessing. But in retrospect it became crystal clear that Trump and his administration were broken before they started.

Some who knew Trump before he ran for president approached him with considerable caution. One example is former secretary of homeland security Michael Chertoff, who previously had served as a federal prosecutor. Chertoff told me: "I've observed Trump one way or another over many years. When I prosecuted organized crime, he was in bed paying off the mob. I viewed him as corrupt, narcissistic, and overly selfish. And it was pretty clear from the campaign he was going to appeal to ethnic prejudice. So I can't say I was surprised."

For some, the penny drop moment came during the campaign. Former Bush chief of staff Josh Bolten, now CEO of the Business Roundtable, said what he noticed was "the unpredictability, the lack of careful thought, the impulsiveness, the egotism. Those were all very prominently on display, even before he started running for president, but they were very much on display during his presidential primary run. So I was worried about the administration. Starting when it looked like he might win the primary."

Andrew Card, another former Bush chief of staff and former transportation secretary, also spotted warning signs during the campaign. Card is from New Hampshire and noticed the signs during that state's famous "first in the nation" primary process: "The expectation in New Hampshire had been you had to show up, you had to come to my town, and you might have to come to my living room and talk with me. And so we don't want big rallies, we don't want big, staged events. We want to test you under all kinds of circumstances where people are angry that you showed up or thrilled that that showed up or that you're going to have to listen to them for a little bit, not just tell you a story, and Donald Trump refused to play that game. And in fact, I think that he may have only spent one night in New Hampshire during the whole campaign. He would fly in in his plane, go out, do a big rally, give a speech, but he really was never tested by interacting up close with voters."

During the campaign Card was asked by a television interviewer whether he considered Trump to be a real Republican. His answer was clear and brilliantly insightful: "I don't know. I don't think he's really well grounded in any philosophical view about what it means to be a Republican. I think he's a member of the Narcissus Party. And by definition, there's only one member."

As a Capitol Hill staffer for Texas representative Michael McCaul, Miles Taylor saw Trump from the perspective of a committed Republican. Later, after serving in senior positions in the administration, Taylor became so disaffected with Trump that he wrote the famous "Anonymous" critique of the president that ran on the op-ed page of the *New York Times*. But long before Trump was even a candidate, he had an inkling there would be trouble:

"In the middle of the 2016 race, I was working on Capitol Hill at the time, on the House side, as the policy director on the House Homeland Security Committee. Michael McCaul was chairman, Paul Ryan was Speaker. And we were in the midst of developing something for Paul Ryan called the Better Way agenda. Ryan wanted to put out an optimistic center-right vision for America's future. Very policy oriented, but also a brand that Republicans could run on for years. He wanted this to be enduring. And I think, frankly, and had it been successful, he would have seen it as the centerpiece of his time as Speaker.

"So there was a tiny handful of us that were working with Speaker Ryan, to develop that document, to develop that plan and that vision. So I was responsible for a component—we're in the middle of working on that simultaneously, you know. Trump is inching closer to winning the nomination. And we're panicking that this guy, not only is he not a Republican, he's not a small 'c' conservative. And so Ryan's Better Way agenda starts to take on increasing importance, at least in our minds. We think, 'Oh, my God, if this guy gets the nomination, we really have to put something out that stands in contrast to what he stands for.' And, frankly, to try to box him in, because Trump was already talking about protectionist policies, anti-democratic policies, not supporting our allies, kind words about our enemies. All these things that he followed through, but that we were worried did not align with where the GOP was.

"So we're frantically trying to finish this document and put it out, really now in hindsight, very foolishly, thinking that releasing some sort of strategy document was going to box Donald Trump in as the candidate. But that's what we thought at the time, is that Ryan would give it to him and say, 'Hey, you run—this is what we stand for. So this is what you better stand for, otherwise our Republican candidates won't be supporting you. And should you win the White House, this is what you need to govern on, because this is what your Republican Congress is going to be operating on as a playbook.'"

For Miles Taylor, the penny, already pretty much in free-fall, dropped finally when Donald Trump said the words "Muslim ban": "And I went into Chairman McCall's office that same day, and I said, 'This guy is going to destroy the party, and he's gonna rip the country apart.'"

Marie "Masha" Yovanovitch took her position as the US ambassador in Kyiv, Ukraine, in July 2016. She watched the campaign that would ultimately result in her being pulled into the limelight and celebrated for her courage and character, as did the Ukrainians around her. She told me:

"All of us were watching all of these things [the campaign], including comments, statements made during the campaign, and wondering what they meant. But I think, like many people, I perhaps naively thought that when Donald Trump became president he would adhere to the bipartisan consensus on Ukraine and Russia, and that he would learn about the threats out there, the situation, and everything else. And he would understand, not just about Russia, but about other things like the importance of NATO, etc. Obviously, that was an incorrect presumption. I think the Ukrainians, much earlier than I did, understood exactly who Trump was."

"The reason not everyone picked up how aberrant Trump's presidency would be was partly that Trump, never ideologically consistent, sometimes said something that reasonable people could agree with." California congressman Ted Lieu, a Democrat, recalled at first misreading Trump:

"I remember watching the speech Trump gave on election night, and I thought I could work with him, because he basically talked about infrastructure and veterans—those main themes. He didn't say anything crazy that night, and I actually issued a statement a few days after the election saying, 'Donald Trump won the Electoral College. One of the great things about America is our peaceful transfer of power, and we should give him a chance to govern.'" Still, for Lieu the penny would drop soon enough: "A couple of months later, I concluded I was wrong. Because pretty quickly, he started to say the same insane things he said during the campaign. I actually thought he just said those things during the campaign to get elected—he wasn't serious about it—and it became sort of clear to me that he was serious about the insane things he said.

"What really got to me is it became very clear to me that he didn't care about the truth, and once that happens, it leads us down the road to authoritarianism. So pretty much, by the time the Women's March rolled around, and Inauguration Day, I concluded, maybe a little bit before that, that he was a danger to the Republic."

The work behind the scenes during transitions is not just about making appointments, of course. It also involves getting the president and his team up to speed on vital national issues.

But none of these are regarded as being more important than the most sensitive questions of US national security.

General James Clapper, a career military intelligence officer, had been appointed by President Barack Obama as his director of national intelligence, the top job in the US Intelligence Community (IC). He was among those whose responsibilities included briefing the new president. Clapper described the overall climate as unusual, saying:

"To be honest, I think nobody took President Trump seriously to start with, but then when he became the nominee certainly there are a lot of people who harbored concerns about him. I had senior people in the intel community who implored me not to have him briefed even though that had been the custom and has been for decades." He added that the supercharged atmosphere around the election extended beyond Trump, and that he had even gotten a request from then Speaker of the House Paul Ryan asking that Hillary Clinton not receive the type of briefings candidates for president typically get.

"I certainly harbored what turned out to be the naive illusion that somehow President Trump would change," admitted Clapper. "That he would grow into the job, would rise to the occasion, whatever phrase you want to use. And I believed that up to the last minute, even though the transition was pretty ragged, and regrettably, the incoming team, which kept turning over, and blew us off, basically. They didn't want to hear anything. They thought, it seemed, that we were all incompetent and didn't know anything.

"So, when I briefed him in early January, I tried to appeal to his higher values, if you will, and tell him what a national treasure he was inheriting in the form of the national Intelligence Community and the men and women standing by to serve him, and all the difficult decisions he'd have to make. He kind of blew it off; he was being transactional since what he really wanted from me was a public rebuttal of the [Steele] dossier, which, of course, I couldn't and wouldn't do. And I told him that."

(The Steele dossier was a collection of raw intelligence on the ties between the Trump campaign and the government of Russia. Commissioned by the private investigation firm Fusion GPS on behalf of the Clinton campaign as a piece of opposition research, the report had been prepared in mid-2016 by Christopher Steele, a former British intelligence officer.)

Clapper was also surprised to discover that "the first place he's going to visit after the inauguration was—guess where. CIA. So I thought, in my naïve way, 'Well, maybe I got through to him, maybe he got the message. And now he's gonna kiss and make up with the Intelligence Community, at least.' And then came that disastrous speech he delivered [on his first full day in office]. He was okay for a minute or two, but standing [in the lobby] in front of that wall with all the stars on it," said Clapper, referring to the memorial to CIA officers who have fallen in the line of duty, "I think it was 119 stars at the time—it is more now—was a desecration in the minds of intelligence professionals. Not just CIA employees, by the way. I never served in CIA, but I've been around it for forty years. And it was an afront to me and the whole community. And that's when I knew that this is going to be a real challenge for the country."

Intimations of the challenges the administration would face also came early to senior administration officials, as they settled into their jobs and watched how the new administration would operate. Former secretary of defense Mark Esper told me:

"When I became secretary of the army in late 2017, we were on the road to war with North Korea. That is an underappreciated fact. The rhetorical jousting between President Trump and Kim Jong-un in particular, especially with regard to nuclear weapons, was dangerous."

Sometimes these auguries led those preparing to serve in the Trump administration to approach it with a special kind of caution. Fiona Hill, who served in the delicate position of the NSC's senior director for European and Russian affairs from 2017 to 2019, was one of the country's leading Russia experts. She had written a well-regarded biography of Vladimir Putin, and from 2006 to 2009 served as the National Intelligence officer for Russia and Eurasia at the National Intelligence Council. Dr. Hill arrived in an administration already in turmoil just a few months after it started. She described the circumstances:

"By the time I actually got on board, my starting date was April Fool's Day of 2017. From being offered the job in the immediate aftermath of the election in January and through into February, Flynn had been sacked for lying about his meeting with Kislyak. And one of the people that I'd also anticipated working with had hightailed it out of there or was being hightailed out of there. McMaster [the incoming national security advisor] didn't really know anyone in the White House, and I had only met him very briefly at a conference a couple of years before. I didn't really know him. There were also already rumors that [Deputy National Security Advisor] KT [McFarland] was going to be kicked out as well. And within a few weeks after I joined, she was nominated to be ambassador to Singapore, which also didn't pan out. So, there was just a lot of turmoil. And I already understood that I had basically walked myself into a blast furnace."

Hill admitted that "I actually kept the box that I brought with me into the office under the desk, in anticipation that I might be leaving precipitously, at any second. But I thought that while I was there, for the moments that I was there, I would do my best to work with everyone else, just as I'd already committed to, and I would try to see what we could do."

Later she, like Fauci, would become famous for publicly challenging President Trump. But like many others who were less well known, her experience was the same. They all had walked into the same "blast furnace." Many, like her, prepared for the worst. In fact, several went to see former US national security advisor Stephen Hadley. According to more than one person with whom I spoke, he gave them similar advice. He told them that as they entered their job one of the most important things they could do was to establish in their own minds what would compel them to quit. To understand the terms on which they would feel compelled to exit, so they were prepared for that eventuality should it arise.

Fiona Hill, as formidable a public servant as I have ever encountered, was prepared. And, as it turned out, because Donald Trump was the man he was and his administration was the threat to the United States it ultimately became, she had to be.

CHAPTER TWO

The Snake

Here at our sea-washed, sunset gates shall stand

A mighty woman with a torch, whose flame

Is the imprisoned lightning, and her name

Mother of Exiles.

—EMMA LAZARUS, "THE NEW COLOSSUS"

IN HER TYPICALLY brilliant, well-argued dissent to the majority opinion in the case of *Trump, President of the United States, Et Al. v. Hawaii, Et Al.*, Justice Sonia Sotomayor cited a long list of incidents during Trump's presidential campaign in which he pledged a "total and complete shutdown of Muslims entering the United States."

One incident cited by Justice Sotomayor was Trump's quoting, at a campaign rally, the lyrics to "The Snake." Based on a poem by civil rights activist Oscar Brown, the song was originally recorded by soul singer Al Wilson in 1968. Once Brown's family learned of Trump's use of the song to advance his ethno-nationalist, anti-immigrant agenda, they sought an injunction to stop him using the lyrics. But, Trump being

47

Trump, continued to recite the lyrics, often in front of rally crowds who fed off his hatred of foreigners, particularly those with brown skin.

The lyrics tell the story of a half-frozen snake who implores a woman to take him in. She does so, and while holding him to her breast he gives her a deadly bite. Dying, she asks why he did it—she had saved him. The song goes:

"Oh shut up, silly woman," said the reptile with a grin,
    "You knew damn well I was a snake before you took me in."

To Trump and his supporters, the snake represented foreigners, especially those of color, who were entering the country and who were, in their view, poised to destroy it. Of course, there are snakes—and then there are snakes. On the issue of immigration and the related issues of racism and nationalism, the Trump administration was a nest of vipers. And within the nest, other than the president there was one snake more feared, more poisonous, and in his colleagues' view more slippery and lethal than all the rest. Having served Trump from his first campaign through to his post-presidency, this man is his longest-serving close advisor who is not actually a member of the Trump family: Stephen Miller.

Keeping out immigrants—especially Muslims, Latinos, and other people with brown skin—was Trump's signature issue from the moment he descended the long escalator into the lobby of Trump Tower in Manhattan to announce he was running for president. On that day, June 16, 2015, Trump's long-shot candidacy made news, not just because a B-list reality television star was announcing his run for the presidency, but because of an unscripted comment he made to the crowd.

(A crowd that according to former Trump campaign aide Corey Lewandowski included actors paid to be enthusiastic onlookers.)

Trump said: "When Mexico sends its people, they're not sending their best. They're sending people that have lots of problems, and they're bringing those problems with us [sic]. They're bringing drugs, they're bringing crime, they're rapists. And some, I assume, are good people." It was no accident that Trump made this casual abuse of Mexicans the centerpiece of his first moment on the political stage. It spoke volumes about who Trump was and the kind of national leader he sought to be.

At that moment, Stephen Miller, the slim young Duke graduate perceived as a rising star among the fringiest part of the American right-wing media, the man one Trump cabinet secretary described to me as "the embodiment of everything that was wrong with the Trump White House, the worst of the worst," was working on the staff of Senator Jeff Sessions of Alabama. But in Trump, Miller saw a candidate who seemed as committed as he was to the goal of stemming the tide of immigration into the United States and preserving what he saw as America's "culture." He was one of the Trump campaign's first staffers, joining the team in January 2016. At that time he was thirty years old.

What Miller meant when he spoke of "culture" was the culture a white male hierarchy had long sought to impose upon America. Although he was descended from immigrants and later renounced by family members for forgetting that legacy (much as Trump, another self-hating descendant of immigrants, would downplay the fact that both his mother and paternal grandfather had come to America from overseas), Miller embarked on the path of intolerance very young.

In his Santa Monica, California, high school yearbook he quoted Theodore Roosevelt, saying: "There can be no fifty-fifty Americanism in this country. There is room here for only 100 percent Americanism, only for those who are Americans and nothing else." In college at Duke, Miller organized Islamo-Fascism Awareness Week, appeared on right-wing cable television shows, and wrote in his final column for a school publication that he was "a deeply committed conservative who considers it his responsibility to do battle with the left."

In his early years in Washington, Miller was a staffer for Congresswoman Michele Bachmann, herself a onetime presidential candidate with far-right-wing views. Later, he briefly joined the staff of Rep. John Shadegg of Arizona before he joined that of Senator Sessions. These were formative years. Sessions was strongly anti-immigration. Miller helped him lead the opposition to legislation that would offer a path to citizenship for 11 million undocumented immigrants. The Sessions faction eventually lost the vote in the Senate. However, in part thanks to circumstances and in part thanks to continuing opposition from Miller and his allies, the bill was never brought to the floor for a vote in the House.

While on Sessions's staff, Miller had established relationships with the senator and other advisors, such as Gene Hamilton. Hamilton, another young Sessions staffer, would ultimately play a central role in developing and promulgating many of the most odious Trump immigration policies, including the Muslim ban and separating children from their undocumented immigrant parents at the border. In his Senate office job, Miller had also connected with Steve Bannon, who at the time was running Breitbart News, and who supported Sessions's views on immigration.

Soon after, Bannon encouraged the Trump campaign to utilize Miller as a speechwriter. During the campaign his duties grew, including periodically warming the crowds at Trump rallies with chants of "Build the Wall!" A February 2020 *New Yorker* profile of Miller by Jonathan Blitzer recounted how deeply invested he was in the campaign, on a personal, passionate level:

> In August, 2016, at a rally in Phoenix, Trump delivered a policy speech on immigration, written by Miller. It was typically raucous and aggressive, full of racist fearmongering, but it also contained a detailed blueprint. "Our immigration system is worse than anyone realizes," Trump began.

As Trump enumerated the anti-immigration policies he advocated, according to the *New Yorker* account his message reached Miller on a deep level. He would later recount to the *Washington Post* that "it was as though everything that I felt at the deepest levels of my heart were now being expressed by a candidate for our nation's highest office."

"He's Gonna Rip the Country Apart"

In one of Trump's speeches he discussed the idea of a Muslim ban. As noted earlier, the speech sounded alarms for Miles Taylor, who saw the dangers of the Trump approach for the GOP. At the same time, Taylor thought, "He's not gonna win. But who's advising from a national security standpoint? Who can get him to backtrack, because this is likely unconstitutional. So the idea of a Muslim ban was absolutely patently insane. And just so damaging in its rhetoric.

"McCaul, I think the next day, reached out to Rudy Giuliani, who he knew was informally advising Trump, and basically said the same thing to Rudy. 'Hey, we got to get real people in to give this guy a more coherent national security vision, and walk [him] away from radical statements like the one he just made. Whether he wins the election or not, this is going to be stuff that sticks to Republicans.' Rudy agreed. And they pulled together a small outside group to advise [Trump]. It was Rudy, former attorney general Michael Mukasey, Andy McCarthy from *National Review*, and a couple of others."

Taylor determined to try to steer Trump away from the wildly unconstitutional language toward something more moderate, something the Republican Party could also recognize as consistent with its values. He was determined that "on the immediate question of a Muslim ban this is an absolutely absurd thing to say, and he should never say it again." Instead, Taylor tried to give Trump's team "a strong actual counterterrorism policy focused on militant extremists." Giuliani and other advisors wanted to use that as a hook to go in and brief Trump about other national security issues, "to get him back on the reservation." Within a couple of weeks they went to New York and briefed Trump, and that was the last time Trump used the phrase "Muslim ban." Somewhat to Taylor's surprise, the intervention seemed to have steered Trump off the rocks: "He never said 'Muslim ban' again. We thought, 'Wow, it worked!'"

It had not.

Once Trump won, Stephen Miller was soon appointed to head the White House Domestic Policy Council. While the job comes with an imposing title, it is one that has never had much traction in the permanent competition to gain influence in the White House, especially compared with entities like the National Security Council or the Office of Management and Budget (OMB). But Miller would change that. In the Blitzer article he explained part of Miller's rationale for taking a White House post rather than, say, one closer to the action on immigration, like in the Department of Homeland Security or in the US Attorney General's office alongside Sessions. The most important benefit was closeness to the president himself.

Blitzer quoted a former top administration official who pointed out another advantage of being in the president's immediate circle rather than in a government department: "The rest of us have to testify before Congress. That's a check. If you're going to have your ass hauled before Congress, you're not going to feel comfortable breaking the law. Miller will never have to testify for anything."

Miller's position inside the White House meant he could ignore the normal channels of communication that take place in the US government. Key agencies from the State Department to the Department of Homeland Security were not included in his thinking or given advance notice of his initiatives. Important steps involving legal review were also overlooked. The Trump view, which the president inculcated in those closest to him, was much like his view when he ran his small family business. One of those who worked in the White House characterized it to me this way: "It's my show. I'll run as I want. I'm the president. People will just have to figure out how to get it done." Miller was determined to get it done Trump's way.

Shortly before Trump took the oath of office, Miller began to translate his demons and his legislative impulses into

what would become one of the first, most controversial signature Trump initiatives: an effort to ban the entry of immigrants from certain largely Muslim countries into the United
States. Just as had happened with other transition efforts, the
initiative was not prepared in traditional ways, for instance,
by focusing on the legal issues surrounding the proposed
measure. Instead, Miller emulated his boss, and with Gene
Hamilton (also a former Sessions staffer who was spearhead-
ing transition efforts on immigration) ignored the advice of
career professionals and drafted an executive order entitled
"Protecting the Nation from Foreign Terrorist Entry into the
United States."

The result was, in the words of one senior DHS official,
"an absolute shit show." No one thought to notify DHS in
advance or even consult its top officials. When the order came
down, they had to scramble to respond. But even as they did,
they encountered some weird twists and turns.

One top member of the team at DHS described how
tough it was to deal not just with the contents of the new
executive order, but also with the intrigue surrounding how
it had come into being: "Gene [Hamilton] was telling him
[Stephen Miller] everything. Gene was loyal to Stephen and
their shared vision for immigration restrictions, and not to
anyone or anything else. Which would have been fine if he
had just said that. Or if that was just made known at the beginning. But for some reason he felt compelled to hide it. The
chain of command—from the president to cabinet officials to
their staff—was circumvented. The best example of that was
the travel ban executive order. He had written it, worked on
it, and, like Stephen, he knew it was coming out. And when it
came out, it surprised everyone. And Gene played along. Like
it was a surprise."

Within hours, it became clear that Trump's executive order had thrown the entire US immigration system into chaos. Crowds of angry travelers who had been issued visas or granted refugee status were turned away. Protestors gathered at airports across the country. Riot police were dispatched.

Olivia Troye was a national security professional who had begun her career in the wake of the September 11 attacks, serving in the Baghdad office of Ambassador L. Paul Bremer, who oversaw the Coalition Provisional Authority. She later served in the Pentagon. At the beginning of the Trump administration, Troye was an official in the DHS Office of Intelligence and Analysis. She remembered her initial reaction to the announcement of the travel ban executive order: "When he got elected, I kept hoping that during the transition between that and Inauguration Day, the campaign rhetoric and the way he was speaking about immigrants and Mexicans and everything like that would change."

Troye wished that once he took office, "Donald Trump would become presidential, because I kept hoping the switch would flip and he would become actually a leader in that role sitting in the Oval Office." She held her breath through the inauguration formalities until "literally right out of the gate, we got word of the travel ban, the restrictions, the travel restrictions— an executive order that hits with no real guidance on how to implement it. No definition of what it is. I think part of it was written in a way that didn't quite make sense."

It was so incoherent that it was susceptible to all manner of legal challenges, which immediately hobbled the order's effectiveness: "I do remember that they were playing catch-up with it, and in the end on how to rewrite it and reissue it. I think they kind of updated along the way, because they're seeing the lawsuits that are about to come in." At which point the penny dropped for Troye: "To me, I was like, 'This is how it's gonna be.' And then I just remember watching the chaos at the airports. And none of us at DHS had any idea what the heck was going on."

Elizabeth Neumann described the confusion and uncertainty created by the order: "Custom and Border Patrol's lawyers are looking at this going, 'I think this applies like immediately,' but they don't know for sure. They had to get everybody on the phone. Figure out how to handle certain cases. It was completely avoidable chaos, trying to rapidly implement and communicate to the operators on how to handle this.

"One of the key criticisms about the travel ban was that it created chaos at the airports. And spokespeople for the Trump administration maintained that was not true. I don't know the ground truth. There were competing stories. We were getting different accounts from CBP [Customs and Border Protection] and from the offices of members of Congress who went to their local airports. But, for me, aside from the horrible policy itself, the bottom line was: it was just a badly designed rollout. Nobody with any experience in government would say, 'Hey, I have a great idea. Let's take an organization with like, fifty-five thousand people and rewrite the rules for them overnight.' You cannot communicate to a workforce that size through a tweet. It doesn't work, right? There are systems in place to communicate but they don't work instantly. There are trainings and protocols to update. Meanwhile, you have lawyers going, 'Technically, we have to do this now. We're in violation of the executive order if we don't implement it now.' So we had to scramble. We had to make it work. What I recall from that weekend was a lot of phone calls with lawyers."

From his perspective on Capitol Hill, Miles Taylor saw the impact of the order on the Republican caucus: "The House Republican leadership were, of course, furious. Furious that the White House hadn't consulted us."

Compounding the problem for Republicans on the Hill was the fact that the order itself was a legal shambles. Taylor instantly knew it could not possibly work: "The second I read the text, I could tell that it was going to be unconstitutional, because it essentially applied to people who already had green cards in the United States. It applied to people who already have a right to enter the country. And now we were suddenly denying them that right. I mean, it was just manifestly poorly written, poorly considered, and broken."

To make matters worse, Taylor quickly realized that the leads at the DHS had never seen the order prior to its publication: "As [Secretary] Kelly and [DHS Chief of Staff] Nielsen would later tell me, they had gotten no heads-up from the White House. And so, look, it's the Homeland Security secretary that's supposed to be implementing this order. And he's not even aware of what's happening. And Nielsen and Kelly were on a plane somewhere. I think they were headed to New York. Maybe [Kelly] was making a speech or something. And that's kind of when they found out. And they had a big dustup with the White House."

In the following days, Taylor became the conduit between the disgruntled DHS and the White House: "Kelly's message back to them was 'You could have prevented all this catastrophe if you had come to me in my department first, which is responsible for these types of things. And we could have helped you craft a more appropriate order to keep terrorists out and let freedom-loving people into the country.' But, of course, they didn't do that. And it did demonstrate Stephen [Miller]'s power, a factor that continued throughout the entirety of the administration."

"Kelly was not happy," Elizabeth Neumann confirmed. "But in the, in a crisis, he digs in and works the problem. Nobody was happy. It was 'Are you kidding me? Why would you guys do this to us? Why wouldn't you give us a heads-up?' I heard later that in Stephen's mind, the surprise element was important because then 'terrorists' couldn't plan to sneak in at the last minute. And you're just like, 'Do you have any understanding about how we do terrorist watch lists?' [Miller] really didn't. It was not his area of expertise."

A Dystopian Fantasy

Neumann realized that Miller was in the grip of a dystopian fantasy: "Stephen made up this false narrative, that we have all these terrorists coming into the country. And therefore we have to catch them by surprise, otherwise, they'll book their ticket; they'll get here before the deadline. It just boggles the mind how naive and inexperienced he was. Their process was so bad. It was really kind of a mess, especially those early days before Stephen quite figured out how to accomplish what he wanted to accomplish. And he was so fearful of telling anybody his plans. So he never asked for help. He was his own worst enemy at being able to get any of his agenda done."

When the secretary of the Department of Homeland Security and other colleagues went to the White House to better understand the situation, they were told to get with the program, that this was the "new world order."

Court challenges followed. The process of meeting the legal criteria that Miller and Hamilton had ignored led to the effort being bogged down in the courts for a year and a half. It was during this period that officials of DHS, at State, and elsewhere in the government began to do what they could to defuse what several characterized to me as the "fundamentally racist" origins of the executive order. US law bans religious discrimination as a reason for denying entry into the country. But it does allow the president to act to protect national security. So an alchemy took place that made a repulsive piece of legislation somewhat less odious. In concert with the courts, officials worked to come up with national security criteria that could enable something like the original executive order (which ended up being redrafted two more times) to take effect. Like the philosopher's stone, which in ancient legend could be used to turn base metals into gold, there was something about the often dreary, often invisible work of government. The touch of the "deep state" that could turn the repulsive and unconstitutional into government policies and actions that were at least legal and more morally acceptable.

Process was at the core of it. As chief of staff at DHS, Kristjen Nielsen's core responsibility was managing that process. In the eyes of those working with her, it made a big difference.

"Kristjen was really good at letting you know the priorities without revealing the chaos she was enduring and the depth of the pressure she was under. She tried to protect us from how bad it really was," recounted Elizabeth Neumann who was then serving as assistant secretary of homeland security for counterterrorism under Nielsen. "I remember fairly early on in my tenure as assistant secretary, sitting down with my team to understand the back-end process that determined who could be eligible for travel restrictions. After briefing her on the project plan for the second review, she said, 'That takes too long. You need to speed it up, because I'm getting pressure' and 'We got to get this done really quickly.'

"So, while she was receiving heavy pressure to finish the review, and identify the countries that were deficient in their identity management and information sharing practices and eligible to be banned, she never once told me, 'You've got to add countries to the list,' which is what the president was telling her. I didn't find that out until I left. She let the team do the work based on the data, based on objective criteria. I don't know if she was doing this on the advice of counsel, or because she is a lawyer herself. She certainly understood the scrutiny this program was going to get. But she also was just a big believer in letting the work of government work."

Since the executive order was essentially unprecedented— it lacked definition except for the broad and ultimately useless notion of "Muslim countries"—it required a lot of back-and-forth to translate it into something legally enforceable, let alone acceptable. Neumann was in the middle of what she called the art of the process:

"This is where the art comes in. We were trying to be productive, to manage the process not as Miller may have wanted it, but as it should be done. There's no predefined level or cut-off in law at which a travel restriction is required—it's all discretionary. So we used the argument that we shouldn't penalize a country if we, the US government, cannot provide technical assistance to help that country, to help them overcome whatever the deficiency was. We have limited people that can do this kind of work. And we have limited dollars to help with technical assistance. So we argued, 'Let's only penalize those for whom we have the ability to provide technical assistance so they can get off the list by the next time we review them.' So that argument was fairly successful, especially among our State Department or DOD colleagues. I found out later, after I had left, that Stephen was unhappy that there weren't more countries on the list."

But Miller had deliberately isolated himself from the process by taking a White House, not a cabinet office, job. "And he knew enough and was warned by counsel that he shouldn't have his fingerprint on the mechanics of what we set up," Neumann said.

A senior official within DHS described translating Trump's whim into a goal the DHS could reasonably embrace: "The goal was not to punish anyone, in my mind. The goal was to have a repeatable, transparent, legal process whereby we could do our role as the Department of Homeland Security, and understand who was traveling into our country. I mean, that's in the Homeland Security Act. One of the mission sets here is understanding who and what is coming in our borders. That's why we do screening."

There are different memories of how the interagency process worked. According to the same official: "We had to pull the State Department a little bit kicking and screaming, because it was, if nothing else, extra work for them." Also, everyone could see the task was a nightmare, and no one really wanted to own it: "I think, as we all saw, when something went wrong somewhere, nobody else wanted to be associated with it."

For many of the countries the DHS focused on, the usual assumptions about who their citizens were didn't necessarily apply, the official realized: "We base travel on a passport credential. But if you're coming from a country that, despite international law, fails to report lost and stolen passports to Interpol, and you show up with a passport, nobody has any idea if the passport is real. It's that simple. How do we know?

Or to take that one step further, there were still countries that weren't sending us exemplars of their passports. So now you don't know what a real one looks like. And oh, by the way, that country also is not reporting lost and stolen [passports] . . . Okay, well, this country has no idea who this person is. How is there a way we can figure out who this person is? Right? Are they who they say they are? And so it required a lot of data, and then a lot of analysis from State."

Tom Shannon was acting secretary of state when the travel ban dropped. A career Foreign Service Officer, one of the most respected of his generation, he had decades of State Department experience serving administrations from both parties. His philosophy aligned very much with that embraced by Nielsen and the others grappling with the problem of translating an odious executive order into a sensible way to protect US national security. Or at least as sensible a way as possible under the circumstances.

"We were still very committed to this idea that our purpose was to make government work," said Shannon, "and to ensure that our elected officials had the capability of governing, and giving the American people what they had asked for in an election. And because most of the people coming into the Trump administration had very little government experience, and very little understanding of how you get from A to B, that gave us a degree of influence, that we could help educate people while we tried to guide them and direct them. And the early executive orders, the early travel bans were examples of this, because they were written in the White House. And not widely shared. But the White House counsel's office did share them, for instance, with the legal advisor's office in the State Department. So the acting legal advisor would call me up and say, 'Hey, we have an executive order here, you need to take a look at it.' And so we would sit down and look at it and realize, 'Oh, my God, this is going to be a disaster.' Not because we disagree with the policy, but because the structure of it, the way it was written and presented just missed a whole lot."

Shannon continued: "A perfect example is the early executive orders. For instance, limiting refugees from certain countries, or insisting that refugees needed to be vetted in a completely different way. Because the people who are writing these executive orders did not realize that our refugee programs were global. And those programs were operating twenty-four hours a day. And they were generating refugees who were eligible for travel to the United States, and who, guess what, were either coming out of camps or selling their homes and their possessions, and going to the embassies or wherever to pick up their travel documents and their passports, and were getting on airplanes. And at any one moment, there were hundreds of the people in motion, or in the air somewhere about to arrive in New York or Los Angeles. And these people had to be dealt with."

Shannon grasped that the administration's blanket new approach threatened to stifle all the ongoing refugee and immigration programs at a stroke: "The administration announces that people coming from certain countries need to be vetted in a special way or need special visa processing, like Iran. Then you end up with a scientist from Cambridge University in the UK, who's lived in Great Britain all his life but still has an Iranian passport, suddenly is stopped at Boston airport and told he can't go to the conference at Harvard. And that person calls Cambridge and Cambridge calls Boris Johnson and Boris Johnson calls somebody, and so there was a whole effort that had to be made to kind of fix what was coming out of the White House. And at that time, in the very early days, General Kelly was at DHS. And I knew Kelly well, from his days first as Leon Panetta's military aide, but then as US Southern Command combatant commander. And so Kelly and I would get on the phone and say, 'Okay, how are we going to figure this out?' So we would create these small working groups, and his staff and my staff would then try to fix what was being presented. So that was a kind of immediate and everyday example of how we tried to fix things."

Invariably, the process did not always run smoothly. It was hugely resented by the government professionals. In the wake of the first travel ban, over one thousand State Department Foreign Service Officers registered their discomfort with the initiative. Via what is known as the department's "dissent channel" (ostensibly a safe space to allow officials and employees at State to express their views), they condemned the exclusion of people by religion, and argued that the program would do damage to America's international standing.

Shannon described what happened next: "You'll recall that the then press secretary, Sean Spicer, went out and in response to a question said, 'Anybody that doesn't like the policy can leave.' That was not, of course, the kind of thing you want to hear. So, I had to work backwards with the White House. I had to convince them that the department was prepared to do what the president asked of it. But that we had a responsibility to listen to what our officers had to say. And that the whole dissent channel process was designed to allow that to happen, without requiring any kind of a break in obedience or discipline, or without requiring resignations or firings—that people could express an opposing point of view and still stay within the chain of command. The White House didn't understand that."

The Triumph of the Process

When Rex Tillerson was confirmed as secretary of state, he worked closely with Kelly and with Secretary of Defense James Mattis. They in turn urged dialogue up and down the chain within their departments. "Our counselors," according to Neumann, "were talking to the secretary of state's counselors. John Kelly [and later Nielsen] was talking to Tillerson, as they were supposed to. Everybody's talking and getting on the same page. And they would agree together on whether we should change this or that and intervened to resolve debates. Of course, I think if it had been up to Kelly, Tillerson, and Mattis nobody would have received travel restrictions, but that was not an option."

Olivia Troye recalled that getting the Intelligence Community to cooperate was a challenge. She had their trust because of her background in the IC. She knew how they thought. And she used that to help overcome their fear of being tainted by the stink that had almost immediately attached to the travel bans.

"I end up having a conversation with one of the IC agency heads," said Troye. "It was a tense conversation between me and them, and I say to them, 'You can either do this with me or we can do it alone. But I promise you, it's going to be that much worse. If you don't help me, if we don't figure out how to set criteria and use factual information that is applicable to whatever this is going to be, this is going to get written and we will probably be in a worse situation. If we don't figure out how, if you don't come together and help. And so you need to be in these meetings; because of that you need to be participating with me. And I will certainly tell you what I see that's happening behind the scenes, and then we can figure out how we're going to navigate the situation in a factual, intelligence-based manner.'

"Basically, I just say to him, 'This is going to happen with or without you. And it is better for the country and for our national security if we figure out how we're going to deal with this, right?' Because at the beginning, all these people, they really just wanted to wash your hands of it and it be like, 'Your problem, DHS. Good luck.' And I'm like, 'Well, no, it's not. It's not. It's not just a DHS problem, because we're going to use your intelligence. And it's going to get spun in a way that you're not going to like.'"

Elizabeth Neumann described later aspects of the approval process, when the agencies would put together their recommendations via a formal procedure and then Miller's team, the people he trusted, would have a closed-door session and try to get the list changed. The agencies, however, learned to then get lawyers involved to mitigate the White House cabal's effect.

She explained: "Determining the penalties [i.e., travel restrictions] for a deficient country was supposed to be facilitated by the NSC and include the perspectives of any agency with equities [State, DOD, Treasury, IC, etc.]. And we weren't seeing the NSC do anything. The lawyers made them backtrack and have a meeting with an agenda that was chaired by the National Security Council, as opposed to Stephen, to evaluate and make them agree to what eventually was put into the proclamation.

"Since the travel ban had already been in front of the Supreme Court, DOJ wanted everything to be rigorously documented. The team at the solicitor general's office spent an enormous amount of time testing our assumptions, criteria, and methodology to ensure it was as legally sound as possible.

"I quietly flagged my concerns to my counsel, who flagged to DOJ and the solicitor general. I would give them the questions, they would give it to the solicitor general, and his office would talk to the White House counsel. And then certain things got changed based on that. Now, I don't think that fully disrupted everything, but it at least injected and forced certain parts of the government to do what they were supposed to do, like, look at this holistically.

"For example, what if we're going to consider banning Eritrea, which doesn't even have a credit card system that works in their country? And we're asking them to share data electronically? So we asked, 'Can we try to make our actions a little bit more relevant to where they are in their development? Are we offering them technical assistance? Are we giving them money so that they can do this because, clearly, if the country doesn't even have a functioning credit card system, their technological capabilities for routine information sharing are limited.' When [Mike] Pompeo became secretary, I have to admit it became harder. His people were less engaged."

During that process, a battle took place as Trump and Miller and their allies pressed to make the barriers more onerous. Trump regularly railed against provisions that weakened the order and called for more countries to be named. Periodically—as was well depicted in the excellent book *Border Wars* from *New York Times* correspondents Julie Hirschfeld Davis and Michael D. Shear, and echoed in my own research for this book—Trump would demand that immigrant flows from "shithole countries" (to use his term) be stopped. He would rail against flows from places like Somalia and Haiti, and direct officials to increase the numbers from places like Norway.

Miles Taylor, by then deputy chief of staff for DHS, recalled the meeting: "I was in a meeting with Trump in the

Oval [Office] once where he literally told the secretary, 'I want you to admit people from Denmark, Finland, Iceland, Norway, and Sweden'—he named the Nordic countries. 'And I want you to stop all immigration from Haiti, Somalia, Ethiopia.' And he listed a whole bunch of other countries. It was unmistakable. The first list was white, blond-haired people. The second list was brown, poor people. That was the most naked expression of his bigotry that I'd ever seen. You can't come to any other conclusion."

Meanwhile, Stephen Miller would seek to bludgeon cabinet officials into action, often sidestepping the traditional government chain of command altogether. As he realized his plans were being thwarted by the agencies, he would identify sources who could act as spies and advance his interests, or let him know when his directions were being ignored. More senior officials regularly pushed back against his interventions, with the president or the White House chief of staff (especially later when DHS secretary Kelly, who was not a Miller fan, became Trump's second chief of staff).

Fortunately for those seeking a more reasonable course of action, the courts laid out clear parameters that had to be followed. Ultimately, those parameters were used to slow the process by delaying implementation of the executive order and by narrowing its scope. One delaying tactic, for example, was to poll embassies worldwide about their perception of threats.

In addition, certain elements of the ban Trump wanted were seen by officials at DHS, State, and the Department of Defense as actually being counterproductive to national security. For example, Trump and Miller wanted the ban to include countries like Iraq and Afghanistan, which would have made it next to impossible to aid or support individuals who had played a central role in US military and intelligence operations there.

One senior official who was in some of the meetings in the Pentagon said: "Mattis felt very strongly that the measures we were putting in place there, along with State, were already well above the baseline, and that based on our unique insight we knew that in certain cases there didn't need to be immigration restrictions placed on that country. And Miller couldn't accept that. He was baffled by it. But, again, they were pretty much boxed in. They were going to have to go to war with these much more experienced cabinet secretaries than their advisors if they wanted to overturn those recommendations."

Troye, who had served in Baghdad in the office of the Coalition Provisional Authority in the early days of the Iraq War, had the trust and shared the concerns of many in the Pentagon and the Intelligence Community. "Firstly," she said, "we were worried. We were worried a lot about what that would mean on the ground when you do such a thing. These are the people who are helping our soldiers and intelligence officers on the ground and their translators. Think about the message you're sending: we want you to continue to support our troops and our intelligence officers on the ground. Think about it from that angle on what you're saying, to an entire population in a country. And that was my perspective—what I would say in meetings, right. Think about the grave danger that you were about to put most Americans around the world in a lot of these countries that were working very closely [with us] on terrorism, like counterterrorism efforts, and other places. How would that make you feel if you're a person, and you're saying to them, 'You're not welcome in my country, and we can't really explain to you why, or give you a temporary visa, for that matter'?"

The threat was not just to serving Americans abroad but to the next generation of potential US supporters and allies: "Think about what that means for the pipeline. We're seeing this now, actually. We're seeing a lot of it with the pipeline on translators. We had to really weigh in and be like, 'So what are you going to do with these Iraqi translators?' You need to move those Afghan translators out of there who have spent their entire life navigating and helping our troops. I had a translator in Baghdad that really helped me through a lot when I was there. I think about those people who basically were given a carrot and promised refugee status, and that would protect our lives in exchange, knowing the grave danger they were in. All the things that stopped. There are thousands of people in that queue still waiting today."

On another occasion during the process, Trump floated the idea of adding all of Latin America to the travel ban. When he first recounted this to his team, Secretary Kelly, almost dumbfounded, said: "We're talking about apples and refrigerators here. He just doesn't get it."

Taylor looked back on the entire process and remembered the constant struggle between Miller and the agencies. "Stephen wanted to use every single lever possible to reduce immigration from poor countries as much as possible. And then Trump was willing to hop on that bandwagon. So Stephen really drove the train on the travel restrictions. And I'm sure he went to Trump and said, 'This is the way to start keeping people out.' It wasn't driven by national security concern. I don't think that was their motivation, when they had to rewrite the executive order and issue it. It fell to the bureaucracy to determine which countries should be designated and which shouldn't. And that's the first real fight that I had in the administration. There were people like Stephen and others at the White House who said, 'The president expects a big list to come back. You know, there's these initial countries that are being designated because Congress already said their terror concern, but he's expecting a much bigger list. So you guys better come back with a big list!'"

Taylor saw the exhaustive process unfold: "State Department went to every single country in the world and said, 'You must provide us baseline information on how you handle counterterrorism, passports, security, etc.' And we're going to rank all countries in the world based on how they provide that information. The countries that ended up in the final 'restrictions' were pretty much the same countries from the start, because they're the ones that just don't cooperate with the United States. North Korea was on there. Venezuela declined to provide the United States the information. Yemen. You go down the list.

"There were a couple that were added, of course, that were non-Muslim countries, because they simply wouldn't cooperate with the State Department."

But for Trump and Miller the list was never huge enough: "We never heard the end of it. Whether it was Kelly or Nielson that would go in for other meetings with him, he would bring it up, apropos of nothing and say, 'Why the hell aren't more countries being added to these bans?' And towards the end of my tenure in the administration, once I was chief of staff at DHS, Stephen was calling me personally all the time and saying, 'You guys need to come up with a bigger list for Trump. More countries, or heads are gonna roll.'"

Taylor had regularly to remind Miller that it simply couldn't work that way—that if there was not a rational and justifiable set of criteria to back up why a country had been placed on the banned list, the courts would throw out the entire executive order: "The only reason the Supreme Court upheld it is because they did their own review. And they found that, okay, the decisions on the threat level and the restrictions were largely made based on a bureaucratic process that was demonstrably developed."

A senior DHS insider observed that "[the White House] did not make it easy. For example, Gene Hamilton, the immigration counselor at DHS and former Sessions colleague of Miller's, was placed [at DHS] by the White House. And he and senior members of the team butted heads early in the administration when they would say, 'We have to make sure that the civil servants are the ones doing this impartial analysis.' And Hamilton responded, 'Yeah, but I know the president really, really wants to add,' and he would list a couple of countries that did not even make sense. Those weren't even countries that we could find a rationale to increase vetting to protect America from terrorism. And he would be like, 'Yeah, but I mean we should look at ways to make it work.'"

For reasons such as these, pretty soon Taylor felt that "every decision the administration made was political interference from the White House, rather than letting people do their jobs."

He added: "Stephen had wanted just a bunch of countries to come back. He wanted to see this country banned and that country banned. If there's any hint of a single terrorist ever having crossed their borders, or even if there was not and he and Trump didn't like the look of the people from that country, let's ban them. They wanted something massive and punitive and, let's face it, something not driven by our national security interests as the law and the courts required."

"A Weak-Ass Travel Ban"

The process undertaken and overseen by Kelly and Nielsen, the State Department, and the lawyers had by August 2019 produced a professionally crafted review. It would stand the scrutiny of the courts. But when Trump was briefed on it that month by DHS deputy secretary Elaine Duke, Tillerson, and Mattis, according to Taylor the president "was fucking infuriated." What they delivered to him was a list with the same number of countries they had started with, but with fewer restrictions.

"I remember Elaine coming back from that meeting and saying it was a 'weak-ass travel ban,' and he felt boxed in and he was pissed. But at that point, he wasn't quite ready to overrule his National Security cabinet. And so he went with it, and it went forward," Taylor said.

Secretary Nielsen said, in the end, "once the White House let DHS develop an assessment process that was deliberate and transparent, every embassy knew exactly what was required to have folks travel from their country, they knew exactly where they were on the grading system, and if they were in danger of restrictions. And when we tailored the restrictions, it was no longer a travel 'ban.' We had many tools to say certain people could travel, in certain ways under certain umbrellas, given the threat and what information their countries were sharing. It didn't have to be a hammer or a blunt instrument as the original EO directed—we developed a much finer-tuned instrument to assess the various countries and apply restrictions as needed. After DHS—in conjunction with State—developed the assessment process, we could apply narrowly-tailored sanctions against uncooperative countries such as North Korea and Venezuela. The assessment also enabled restrictions to be removed from countries. A so-called 'travel ban' (especially the initially-directed travel ban) never made sense operationally or from a risk management perspective."

In other words, it worked. Although when the final "ban" was implemented in early 2020, almost no one noticed. Because within just a couple of weeks a much more sweeping ban was initiated for a completely different reason: the advent of the COVID pandemic.

While Trump and Miller had, because of the courts and the intervention of government professionals, lost control of the travel ban process, what remained in Miller's control were the jobs of a number of those who had worked to defang the original executive order. And one by one they were pushed aside.

By late 2018 or early 2019 in the eyes of many, as one senior DHS official from the period put it: "Stephen Miller was the shadow secretary of DHS. He pretty much had all of the control. He would take another full year before he could do almost anything he wanted. There were still some checks there that would prevent the person he would want for a certain position going in there. But he just kept firing people. Like John Mitnick, because as general counsel Mitnick would refuse to sign off on things that he believed were illegal. And so, Stephen's like, 'Okay, you're fired.' And Miller and company put in their own counsel."

Another very senior administration official who was closely involved in all the major battles between Miller's office and the rest of the bureaucracy observed: "Stephen is socially awkward, but he is smart. And he figured out the game pretty quickly, and he figured out the levers. He could figure out who was with him and who was against them. And he survived in a White House that very few people, unless you were related to Trump, survived. So there's a savviness there. But you can't walk away from an interaction with him and not wonder if he's on the spectrum. High intelligence, but can't seem to relate to people, or recognize when it just lacks a certain element of humanity to his personality or his interactions."

The twisted view of how to deal with immigrants, of course, was not limited to the travel ban. Bush DHS secretary Michael Chertoff observed: "I think in DHS, many of the parts worked well. Those that worked best were not particularly political, like TSA, Coast Guard, CISA, etc. But one area that got politicized was the border. And with Trump's desire to emphasize the border as the main thing DHS should be focused on, I think there were some people in, for example, the border patrol and ICE, particularly in the unions, who saw this as an opportunity to loosen the restraints on their activities. There were some among them who liked, if I can use the expression, 'kicking ass.' That posed a challenge, I think, for John Kelly and Kirstjen Nielsen. They reined that in to some extent. But, as you know, Trump kept rotating the leadership at DHS, so that there wouldn't be any consistency."

There was also the matter of Trump's bizarre dream of building a barrier at the border. Trump would offer up crazy ideas in meetings that it was up to the members of his cabinet to shoot down, in part because his White House inner circle would seldom say no to him.

One official present at the Oval Office meetings in which Trump fantasized about how to keep immigrants out along our southern border recounted: "He wanted to do the crazy stuff in his dream, which would be everyone else's nightmare. The border wall would have been one hundred feet high with sharp rotating spikes at the top, painted matte black, so that it heated up in the sun. It was electrified to shock migrants and had devices on it and sharp edges, such that if anyone would fall it would be certain to kill and maim them in a way that would dissuade others from going over it. And then, in the meantime, he wanted to dig a moat as deep as the wall was tall, so it would double its size, and put alligators and poisonous snakes in it to attack people who came in. These weren't jokes. He was serious. This is how he envisioned it."

Trump's cartoon nightmare barrier was not a one-off notion. He would share the idea repeatedly over many years. He was obsessed with a killer fence and a hellish ditch that would run the length of what Trump saw as Fortress America.

Officials learned to turn Trump's black and white, good versus evil cartoon understanding to their advantage when they wanted the president to sign off on what was essentially a dull or routine piece of border kit. "US Customs and Border Protection might come and say, 'You know, this is the anti-climbing feature we bid out fifteen years ago that we really like in the Rio Grande sector. We only have two miles of it.' The fence was glamorized and sensationalized when presented to the president, who was told, 'Your sharpshooter team of border agents just came up with the toughest way to keep people from getting in. It's this superclimb-something feature.' I mean, you had to handle him just the way you would sell a Nerf gun on Nickelodeon to a kid. It's just a piece of plastic with a foam dart that shoots out. But man, isn't it cool. And it's spray-painted neon. And, frankly, you had to go do that on some pretty consequential decisions with him to either get him to do the right thing, or keep him more often than not from doing a bad thing."

Kristjen Nielsen suffered Trump's obsession with building a wall at the southern border: "We must have had thirty discussions about the design of the top of the wall and many more on the overall design. He wanted it to be a very provocative design, whereas DHS had done an extensive amount of analysis to ensure that the wall had an operational purpose as part of a system of systems. But he was always much more interested in the provocative style of it. And a lot of it was not operationally sound. So, for example, he wanted to put spikes on top of the wall, but spikes actually make it easier to crawl up the wall—so operationally that doesn't make sense. Another example—he asked about building a moat, but that would require the moat to be built on the US side, and, arguably, it could put migrants in additional danger when crossing. Operationally, we would then have an additional duty to rescue folks from the moat and they would be on US soil when interdicted. Also, in essence, that would require building three walls (two sides and some sort of structure on the floor/ground to keep the water)—which would not achieve any additional operational objectives and would require resources beyond what was appropriated. We were always trying to go back with pictures and data to say, 'Sir, that design is not going to meet our operational objectives.'

"He wanted to paint it flat black, had to be flat black, and that became somewhat of a sad joke amongst those of us who were part of the conversations. When I was there, I said no to the request repeatedly. It was going to cost ballpark over $2 million on top of an existing contract to paint it, and you'd have to pay to change the contract design. But he kept raising it. His belief was that [painting it black] makes it hotter to the touch to deter climbing. But that's just not accurate. We were instead focused on making the wall an effective barrier and the cost of the paint would be significant. DHS wanted to maximize delivery to areas where a wall could be effective based on operational realities and environmental nuances."

Astonishingly, senior staff had to spend time debating the merits of alligators and moats, one person familiar with their conversations said: "I mean, there's no proof at all that if we had alligators and moats that it would even deter people, because they could just go to another place. It just becomes a little bit of a joke, right?"

Another senior government official described having to painstakingly explain to the president that one reason you cannot build a moat directly next to a wall is that either the wall will fall down or the moat will cave in. It simply didn't make any sense. "Because what you're actually telling me to do is build three walls. And you've got all the problems with all the issues of building on that border to begin with, whether it's personal property, whether it's environmental concern. Now you have to have an even bigger, wider expanse to build this moat. And, by the way, you have to build a moat along the whole border. Or people are just going to go to another part of the area, which is the problem with the wall, too. I mean, the wall will stop people right there, but sure, they're gonna find a way to go somewhere else." This official was struggling to convey what one the former DHS secretary, Janet Napolitano, had pithily said: "Show me a fifty-foot wall and I'll show you a fifty-one-foot ladder." But Trump didn't get it.

Can't You Shoot Them in the Legs?

Another refrain of Trump's with regard to immigrants at the border, said three different top officials with whom I spoke who were familiar with the conversations, was asking, "Can't you shoot them in the legs?" Trump had raised the idea of having US border authorities actually open fire on people approaching the border in an unauthorized place or manner. Nielsen described Trump saying: "'We'll just shoot them in the legs. They'll be fine, but we'll just shoot them in the legs.' So, first of all, it's an absurd thing to say. DHS doesn't have use of force authority or protocols like that. DoD didn't have engagement authority given the circumstances, either, to my knowledge. I'm not sure whether he meant it or not. But there certainly were multiple directions given that he did mean and putting aside the serious moral and ethical questions of comments such as shooting someone in the leg, they often just didn't make sense, weren't operationally sound, and/or weren't within existing authorities or resources."

Another example Nielsen cites, one that contributed to the final breakdown in her relations with Trump and his inner circle during her tenure as secretary of homeland security, was linked to the ultimate Miller-Trump dream: shutting down the border altogether.

"The border closure threat was a big one [reason I left]," she said. "And we got close, frankly, we got so scary close, at least twice." Nielsen attacked the idea from every angle she could think of, and brought in other officials to back her up. "I mean, I even had [US Trade Representative Robert] Lighthizer involved. I was coming at it from the economic perspective, from the security perspective, from the international perspective and operational perspective—there is no way we can shut down the border. It is literally not possible. We don't have enough people to go link up, arm in arm, along the whole border. And I believe the effects would have been devastating internationally and economically—certainly would have put the USMCA at risk—for him to take some sort of formal action to announce it was 'closed.'

"Nonetheless we came dangerously close. There were very heated conversations. Stephen Miller and other senior advisors within the White House and parts of the Justice Department kept telling President Trump that he did have the authority to 'not let people in.' And this was an issue during my whole tenure as Secretary. As early as February, March, after I was confirmed, there was a Cabinet meeting after which I almost quit, because the Attorney General of the United States of America told the president that I had the authority to just quote unquote, 'not let them in.' And that became the refrain the entire time I was Secretary, 'Honey, just don't let them in.' But that's not legal. If they physically touch the United States, they can claim asylum. They have a right to be processed. I can't 'simply push them back'—that goes against our border and immigration authorities. I told him it was not legal—and operationally impossible. But then again, when the Attorney General is saying it is legal in front of the White House staff, the President just thought that I was wrong, that I was wrong on the law. The problem was compounded by the fact that TV commentators and folks outside government had also convinced him that this was something he could do, that he could just not let people in. And I was always trying to be the voice of reason. And he didn't like it."

Tensions continued to build. Then one day, Nielsen was traveling on a mission to Europe to meet with America's Five Eyes intelligence partners. (This was a central part of her DHS job that Trump, in her mind, never fully appreciated—despite the fact that the department had six thousand overseas employees.) Shortly after she landed, she received a message from the White House saying the president wanted her to return immediately to the United States, because "she has to be on the border. The president doesn't understand why she's in England. That's not what she does."

When she flew back, she realized that Miller and the White House team wanted to undertake what she called a "coup," firing a number of top officials within the DHS whom they did not trust, including the head of the Secret Service, the general counsel of the department, and others.

When confronted with the plan, Nielsen responded that while these individuals served "at the pleasure" of the president, she was not going to fire them. In her opinion, they had done nothing wrong, hadn't broken any laws, and were doing an effective job.

Later, in Nielsen's words, the coup de grâce came as she "just finished negotiating these very breakthrough agreements with the Central American countries and Mexico. Mexico, for the first time, had agreed that they were going to start to truly enforce the border on their southern border, and it included a big agreement with Central America on information sharing, law enforcement cooperation and collaboration to stop smuggling and trafficking. We had also agreed to support Mexico by increasing our efforts to prevent guns and weapons from going south across the border from the US. A key component was ensuring more effective and efficient delivery of the aid to Central America that Congress had designated. And he, Trump, lost it. He just lost it—'how dare you give them money'? 'What is the matter with you?' Another example of a reaction that just didn't make any sense. Because anyone who's ever looked at immigration understands there's push and pull factors, and as long as people have a reason to flee their own country, they're going to keep doing it. That's just what's going to happen. So if we don't invest and we don't help them, then we can't achieve our goals. I spent substantial time as Secretary working with the governments of Central America to address the push and pull factors—for example helping encourage e-commerce, working to ensure they received targeted aid from the State Department, supporting efforts to prosecute gangs and cartels to make the communities safer places. It was all so much more complex than just closing the border."

Nielsen was asked to oversee one particularly odious border policy, family separation: "some in the White House and DHS, with the support of the AG's office, wanted there to be an administrative separation policy, which would mean that if you encountered a family, anywhere—at a port of entry or in the interior—and they didn't have a legal right to be there or to stay, you would separate the family, as policy. An example would be when a family presented at a legal port of entry to claim asylum, a policy would direct that they be separated and prosecuted separately. The entire time I was Secretary, I fought that, and I would not let that be implemented. But eventually, the Attorney General issued a 'zero tolerance' policy. Zero tolerance said that we had to enforce the law 100 percent, that is, drastically increase prosecutions against those who crossed between ports of entry—an 'illegal entry'—and we couldn't pick and choose who we upheld the law against. So, if you have a child, you don't have a child, you're married, you're not married, you're young, you're old, the law applies equally and should be enforced by CBP and ICE as law enforcement officers. This was in line with a Presidential Directive Trump had issued early on that said that prosecutorial discretion could not apply to classes or categories of people—so there could not be an overall exemption for adults with children. The separation issue arose, not by direction—there was never any direction under my watch to separate families—but because the resources did not exist within the federal government to quickly prosecute the parents (DOJ's role)while DHS had custody of the children who could otherwise be reunited and processed together. Since we do not put children in jail with their parents in the US, while the parents were in prosecutorial settings, the children remained at DHS. Because of a lack of sufficient resources, DOJ was not able to prosecute parents within 72 hours. After 72 hours, the custody of the children moved from DHS to HHS as required, resulting in the families being separated. It was what I was promised would not happen—that processes and procedures and resources were in place. But it did and was heart wrenching."

Nielsen described months of fighting within the system to resist the separation policy. After the policy was issued, she then worked for weeks to get the resources in place to enforce it. And in her view there was never enough time or resources to make family separation anything other than brutally cruel. She asserted that there were not enough marshals, not enough vehicles to transport those who were in custody, not enough judges to process cases, and so the families were separated for longer and longer periods. The law stated that after seventy-two hours children had to be sent to Health and Human Services (HHS). That made matters more complicated, and considering how the children were being affected by what they were experiencing, even more damaging. This led to more internal conflicts.

For Nielsen, "the very last straw in the meeting, where I did end up leaving, was after I described the new agreements with the Central Americans, I was talking about what a good partner Mexico had agreed to be moving forward. [Trump] was always harping on me that I 'liked the Mexicans too much,' that I was 'too nice to them.' I explained that they were going to execute a specific dedicated border enforcement plan. And he said, 'Well, what percent?' And I said, 'Well, as soon as the [Mexican] National Guard is in place, we think the enforcement percentage will be up, between 30% and 45%, within a few weeks.' And he turns to [White House Chief of Staff] Mick Mulvaney, and says, 'See, this is the problem with her. It should be 100%.' Which is just not possible. We are not remotely able on the US side to enforce 100%—neither are they. True border enforcement must protect vulnerable populations and communities on both sides of the border, address push and pull factors to immigration, and recognize operational realties, resources, and authorities. I know the President would get very frustrated when I spoke about any consideration that was not purely security-related in his mind and would be extraordinarily frustrated that there wasn't a silver bullet, but there isn't—it is much more complex."

Nielsen reportedly replied that it was not possible to achieve that goal given that there were many factors Mexico and the United States did not control. After that point, her effectiveness became compromised, because each discussion with Trump and his top advisors would turn into a struggle. She decided to leave only to discover Trump and those close to him had been planning and working to engineer her exit for some time, to replace her with Kevin McAleenan as acting secretary—someone DHS senior staff say was picked because "he would do exactly what Trump wanted him to do."

Evaluations of Nielsen's tenure, like those of many who served under Trump, will always be tainted by the net impact of the administration's policies, even though some were largely developed by Miller or elsewhere, like at Justice with regard to the family separation policy. Nielsen and her team (many of its key members' accounts have figured in this chapter) had a considerable net positive effect that was largely unappreciated and under the radar. Through their efforts, and others to be highlighted in this book, the worst of Trump and people like Miller was offset, defused, or otherwise moderated.

Nielsen's reward for her diligence was to be fired after a campaign to replace her with a more loyal Trump supporter.

There were, however, greater costs. Many were to the innocent people who suffered terribly as a result of the Trump administration's immigration policies, despite the efforts of some on the inside to ameliorate them. But there were also opportunity costs. Among the most serious were those on the national security front. Olivia Troye described it in the following way:

"There was no real room to focus on domestic terrorism because we really were all focused on the border. I was really passionate about transnational organized crime. So I was hoping that the border thing would help address things like the opioid crisis, or human trafficking, or maybe talk about cartels and threats here, and how these are like transnational organized networks happening here."

But those three-dimensional problems were never given much attention by the principles. They remained stuck on the wrong side of the president's relentless obsession with a wall, with spikes, and a moat filled with snakes.

For Troye it was simple: "I'm from the school of thought that a border wall is not actually going to solve the problems we have, when it comes to the really bad guys we're trying to catch. I mean, look, the people you're claiming are the dangerous people that are coming to our border, and those caravans, are not terrorists. Those are the least of my problems."

CHAPTER THREE

"I Obey,
but I Do Not Comply"

War is peace. Freedom is slavery. Ignorance is strength.

—GEORGE ORWELL, *1984*

FEW AREAS ILLUSTRATE how much worse the events of the Trump era could have been than the relationship Commander in Chief Trump had with his military. Had the most dangerous of Trump's impulses, biases, and misunderstandings translated into action, alliances would have crumbled, enemies would have benefitted, wars would have been fought, war crimes would have been committed, and the military would have in the end become the enforcement arm of an authoritarian government. The military would have been debased and America would have been irreparably damaged.

That is not to say there were not negative consequences to the Trump era. In 2018, according to the Ronald Reagan Institute, 70 percent of Americans had "a great deal of trust and confidence" in the military. By the end of Trump's term the number had fallen to 56 percent. At the same time, Trump's decision to withhold military aid from Ukraine while providing political cover for Vladimir Putin's aggression against it, and seeking to weaken NATO, looks very different and much more reckless in light of Russia's February 2022 attack on its neighbor.

But as each chapter of this book illustrates, the principled, constitutionally based resistance Trump encountered from within his administration to his most dangerous ideas limited the negative consequences of his recklessness.

My Generals

No previous American commander in chief ever viewed the military as Donald Trump did. One senior Pentagon official who served under him said simply: "He thought it was his military. He thought we were toy soldiers he could play with. And he treated general officers like they were brand names that he could flash to his friends and voters so they would take him seriously.

"But that wasn't the worst of it," added this veteran of multiple administrations. "He was erratic. He was uninformed. He did not take advice. And sometimes his ideas were downright crazy. We spent as much time coaxing him away from the brink of really dangerous ideas as we did doing our day jobs."

The examples of Trump's irrational and often deeply strained relationship with the Pentagon are abundant. In *Trump and His Generals: The Cost of Chaos,* Peter Bergen cites many. For example: "When told the capital of South Korea, Seoul, was so close to the North Korean border that millions of people would likely die in the first hours of any all-out war, Trump had a bold response, 'They have to move.'"

Former secretary of defense James Mattis told colleagues he would often get late-night calls from Trump, in which the president fulminated about an issue, often threatening to carry out wildly irresponsible actions. These included, according to a source close to Mattis, the belief that we should immediately attack North Korea (during the early days of his intemperate Twitter campaign against that country). In each of these instances, the cerebral, seasoned Mattis would adopt what became an approach emulated by many in Trump's cabinet. He would hear out the president's late-night rant and then, to defuse the issue, promise to think about it and ask to meet the next day to discuss it. Often by then Trump's "temperature had gone down a few degrees," said one very senior Trump Pentagon official. "Or at least you could invite other people into the room—the calls late at night were often one on one—and ideally some of them were more rational and would help talk the president off the ledge."

One fever nightmare derived from Trump's obsession with the southern border, moat full of alligators and all, went beyond the wish to ask the border patrol or military to shoot at people trying to cross. He floated the prospect of launching missiles at the "caravans" moving up through Mexico toward the United States. "Missiles," said a top military planner, "launched at Mexico!" Trump instructed an aide to call Northcom, the command serving the North American continent, and sought to deploy hundreds of thousands of US troops at the southern border.

He also worked on other unhinged ideas that actually had some support from his inner circle. They ranged from investing heavily in new "more usable" (Trump's own words) nuclear weapons technology to trying to draw down America's troop presence in Europe; then once he got to his second term, withdrawing the United States from NATO (as he told former defense secretary Mark Esper). He was also, of course, impeached for trying to swap Congress-approved US military aid to Ukraine in exchange for dirt on Joe Biden. He actively tried to block efforts to sanction Russia for serial abuses. He wanted to pull US forces from locations worldwide, from Asia to Europe to war zones like Syria.

What is more, throughout his four-year term, he combined a lunatic zeal for bad ideas that would weaken the United States with a profound lack of understanding of what he was talking about or even seeing. Hence, his touching belief that US stealth aircraft were actually invisible—like, say, Wonder Woman's airplane—rather than just nearly invisible to radar, as is the case. Trump also possessed a showman's impulse to regularly use the military as a political prop, as a backdrop for rallies, or as a validator for his policy announcements.

Former senior Pentagon official Kori Schake has even taken to teaching a case drawn from the Trump experience when she lectures senior military officers on the way up the ladder: "When I teach the newly minted general officers, I use the example that Jim Mattis should not have permitted the travel ban to be signed at the Pentagon. That was the White House using the military in support of a phony national security issue. Jim should have said, 'Hey, boss, I don't think that's appropriate here.' And he didn't. But that example shocked the Pentagon into understanding just how much the Trump administration was going to use the military as a validator for their policies."

So, lesson learned. Mattis, while secretary of defense, worked to discourage the president from going to military bases. If he couldn't do that, he wouldn't go with Trump because he knew Trump was holding what were effectively political rallies in front of military audiences who burnished his authority, whether they agreed with what he was saying or not. The military do not have the luxury of disagreeing with the highest figure in the chain of command. So the Pentagon, Schake confirmed, "used the secretary's availability and all sorts of other bureaucratic tools to dampen down the president's ability to roll the military in in support of his policies."

Needless to say, perhaps the most extreme ideas the president floated or considered for using the military came at the end of his tenure. At that time some of his most extreme 2020 campaign advisors, including disgraced former national security advisor General Michael Flynn, recommended he use the military to seize voting machines in the 2020 election. They actually drafted an executive order to implement the idea. This was months after Trump used the chairman of the Joint Chiefs of Staff and the defense secretary as supporting cast in his effort to disband peaceful protests across from the White House. It was also after he began to force out senior defense and intelligence community officials. Replacing them with loyalists gave him additional license to direct the world's greatest military to serve his personal and political goals.

Trump spent five years of his adolescence at the New York Military Academy. According to him, he thrived there. In one interview he reported that "I did very well under the military system. I became one of the top guys at the whole school." Rising to the rank of cadet captain during his senior year, he attributed the promotion to his qualities as a leader. Before his campaign for president had even gained traction, in January 2016 Trump's story was called to question by former schoolmates. The *Washington Post* reported that he got booted out of the "command" job because of hazing that took place on his watch. Even he acknowledged he was a demanding leader. But other former students asserted he was not "paying attention to his other officers as closely as he should," and that in the wake of the hazing the school felt compelled to shift him to a more administrative position.

While Trump swore up and down that he was a great success at the school, the views of fellow students suggest a more complicated story—that of a young man who was entitled, liked to show off his status by disregarding the rules, was often seen with glamorous young women, and was regarded as something of a disciplinary challenge. Fortunately, Trump's father, developer Fred Trump, had cultivated a connection with the commandant of the school, which his classmates would later allege got young Donald special treatment.

Cadet Trump

In the eyes of some of the senior officials who served with Trump, his academy years helped shape his complicated relationship with the military officers he worked with as president. On the one hand, "he felt he understood the military, which he clearly did not," a career officer who had worked closely with Trump told me. On the other hand, he both glamorized the military in the way a teenage boy might, for its shiny buttons and its air of power, but resented it because the core military ideas of discipline and teamwork were and always had been anathema to him.

General James Clapper observed: "He went to military academy when he was in high school. So I think he had a sort of worshipful instinct about senior military officers. And so all of a sudden now that they're all working for him they're his personal possessions, which gets your hackles up to hear them referred to that way." Suddenly, the not-very-good student from the military academy had generals who saluted him. He felt validated by them and he was happy to use them as his props.

Trump, who had never run for president because he expected or even wanted to win, but because he wanted to be, as reported by Michael Wolff, "the most famous man in the world," used all his cabinet picks as adornments to his celebrity. That didn't necessarily mean they lacked talent, but the essential quality they had to deliver was luster. They were the tinsel on Trump's tree. Corporate heavy hitters like Rex Tillerson, or other members of the exclusive club of America's richest citizens, like Commerce Secretary Wilbur Ross, Treasury Secretary Steve Mnuchin, or Education Secretary Betsy DeVos, leant him, in his mind, economic credibility and a certain financial bling in the circles in which he traveled. They compensated for Trump's own very mixed record as a steward of anyone's money.

On national security issues, about which he knew almost nothing, he needed people whose presence could reflect a good light on him. He needed the brass, well shined. In Trump's mind, according to one Trump White House staffer, "that meant generals. Surrounding himself with generals who would say 'yessir' to him meant he was the big man. And it also conveyed a sense of toughness to him. He would refer to them as his 'killers,' at least until he came to realize that most of the generals he settled on were actually thoughtful professionals who, having seen war up close, had no great appetite for it."

One general did not fit that pattern, though, and it's no accident he was the first to sign up for project Trump. Michael

Flynn was the most junior of the generals to join the administration, a three-star general who had been fired from the Defense Intelligence Agency (DIA); Mattis and Kelly were four-star generals. Flynn lasted only three weeks into Trump's term before being fired for making "false, fictitious, and fraudulent statements and representations" about conversations he'd had with Russian ambassador Sergey Kislyak. Yet in a *Frontline* TV interview, *Washington Post* reporter Greg Miller said Flynn "was really important to Donald Trump as a candidate. He was the most senior person in uniform out there campaigning for Trump throughout a campaign in which Trump was having trouble enlisting real, meaningful support from people with stars on their shoulders."

Miller observed that Flynn was "willing to campaign for Trump in a really intense way." Even after Flynn had been kicked out of his job as national security advisor, and before he returned to Trump's side at the end of the former president's term of office, "Trump felt and showed loyalty to Flynn like he did to few people," according to a former Trump NSC staffer. "Part of it was that Flynn was himself intensely loyal. Part of it was that they shared a worldview, including their warm feelings toward Russia. Part of it was that Flynn knew how to make Trump feel like commander in chief. It was the one place where I saw his years of military service really manifest themselves."

Among his former colleagues in the military with whom I spoke, disdain for Flynn was palpable. General Michael Hayden, former director of the National Security Agency and former director of Central Intelligence, said Flynn was "always crazy. There was always something wrong with the guy, and I knew him and worked around him for a long time." After Flynn was fired in 2014 for issues associated with his management style and his "temperament," Barack Obama warned Trump against hiring Flynn, a fact that no doubt elevated Flynn's standing in the incoming president's mind.

Former director of National Intelligence James Clapper, who oversaw firing Flynn, provided more insight: "I had known Mike Flynn. He was an accomplished tactical intelligence officer and had lots and lots of deployed time in Iraq; and especially Afghanistan, maybe too much. I was a co-officiant at his three-star promotion ceremony at the Women's Memorial near Arlington Cemetery. He worked for me for eleven months on the ODNI [Office of the Director of National Intelligence] staff and he was fine. He was the consensus select pick to be director of DIA.

"And I say consensus because DOD's view was represented by Dr. Mike Vickers, who succeeded me as undersecretary for intelligence. He and I both agreed that Mike was the right guy for the job. Well, it turns out he wasn't. And that sometimes happens. You make misjudgments about people. Mike had trouble dealing with a huge agency, made up of mostly civilian employees. Sometimes military guys have trouble transitioning to being boss of a civilian-dominated culture. They're used to giving orders and getting 'yes, sir, yes, sir, three bags full' back. Sometimes with civilians, you give and order and their reaction is 'We'll think about it.' He had trouble adjusting to that culture.

"I started hearing bad things about the morale [at DIA]. So, for different reasons, Mike Vickers and I came to the same conclusion that Mike Flynn had to go. In Mike Vickers's case it was purely insubordination. You know, Flynn just blew him off. And he is the undersecretary of defense for intelligence, the overseer of all DOD intelligence, who has 'authority, direction, and control' over the four intelligence agencies embedded in DOD, as well as all service intelligence. We agreed, and asked Mike Flynn to meet us in Mike Vickers's office in the E Ring in the Pentagon in February of 2014. We told him that we were curtailing his tour as director of DIA to the following summer. The reason for allowing him to stay on for six more months, rather than leave immediately, was so he would get his three years' credit in grade as a lieutenant general, which you need in order to retire and receive retired pay for that grade. The employees would know a date when he was leaving—and it would be a year early. To Mike Flynn's credit, he actually took it pretty well."

Clapper concluded: "What I think happened to him after that was he became an angry man, I think it ate at him that he was curtailed. He started blaming it on Obama, who had never even met Flynn. He was never in the White House. Flynn said it was because of his views on ISIS, which is all bullshit. Then, he emerged at his infamous dinner in Moscow sitting next to Putin. I think he was trying to latch on to any Republican candidate, and managed to click with Trump. When I saw him at the Republican convention chanting "Lock her up," I couldn't believe it. He had turned into an entirely different Mike Flynn than the one I knew. He was just a different guy. Even today, I sort of feel sorry for him and his family, even though he brought all his ensuing difficulties on himself. I also knew he wasn't suited to be the national security advisor. I didn't think he'd last a year, but I thought he'd go longer than twenty-three days."

Former secretary of defense Leon Panetta offered another perspective on Flynn: "I think the first time I crossed trails with Mike Flynn, he was head of intelligence in Afghanistan. I think we were trying to accumulate or put together a report at the time, and he had some criticisms. I didn't feel that it was out of the ordinary. But he generally had a pretty good reputation. In terms of the Intelligence Community, as a matter of fact, when I went back to the Defense Department, he continued to play a role in some of the intelligence areas there as well, and did a pretty good job at the time. But I always knew that Mike had a certain volatile edge to him. There's a lot of people you deal with who sometimes can be emotional or volatile or get angry, fast. That's part of it. But at the same time, they do their job. And Mike did his job.

"I think what happened is that there's a certain ego investment on the part of people who are in jobs where part of it is service to country. Part of it is doing the best job you can to try to protect the nation, and part of it is ego satisfaction. And I think what happened is that the ego part of Mike Flynn took over when he felt that he wasn't respected for what he had done in intelligence. And when a military guy loses respect, he either crawls into a hole, or he gets very angry and tries to get back at you. And I think that's what Mike did."

Whereas Flynn was Trump's "first" general, during the course of the transition Trump had settled on two others for top jobs: marine generals James Mattis as secretary of defense and John Kelly, first as secretary of homeland security and later as White House chief of staff. A fourth general came into the picture in the wake of Flynn's departure, H. R. Mc-Master, who replaced Flynn as national security advisor.

Trump and Mattis had never met when Mattis was called to interview for the job of secretary of defense. The interview lasted one hour. At the time, Mattis was a resident scholar at Stanford University's Hoover Institution. Although he was known as a scholarly and deeply reflective officer, Trump latched on to Mattis's reputation and, uncomfortably for Mattis, a nickname that he deeply disliked: "Mad

Dog." When Mattis was introduced to a crowd for the first time as Trump's nominee, Trump delighted in the fact that the crowd started chanting, "Mad Dog! Mad Dog!" Almost from that point forward, the mismatch—the oil-and-water personalities of the superficial, glib, impetuous Trump and that of his intellectual, measured, deeply principled secretary of defense—began to slowly fall apart. For Mattis "it was just a matter of time." The split finally occurred in 2018, following President Trump's decision to withdraw US troops from Syria and abandon America's long-standing and courageous Kurdish allies.

Kelly did not have the same scholarly reputation as Mattis, but those who had worked with him cited him as a man of character, competence, and patriotism. McMaster, on the other hand, was much more in the Mattis soldier-statesman-scholar mold, an individual who read and thought deeply about the issues he was to face as national security advisor. As such he was as different from Trump as could be imagined.

From the outset of the administration, "alarm bells were going off," according to one senior Pentagon official. In this environment, the generals and their closest aides began to consult with one another, seeking to find a way to bring the new president not only up to speed on the substance of his new job, but also on how the national security apparatus of the US government worked.

Trying Not to Go Off a Cliff

Each of these men had decided to serve, despite questions about the direction of the new administration and concerns about the inexperience of the president. The old question of why they did so would come up and later dog them as their work in the administration grew more challenging. This of course was due to the erratic nature of the president and his often combative, sometimes glib, sometimes irrational style. Panetta speculated as to why: "Out of loyalty to the office, out of loyalty to the country, and in some ways out of loyalty to the politics of the fact that he got elected and he was in office, [as a staffer] you're going to try to do what you can to try to guide [the president] in the right direction. And I think that Tillerson initially felt this way, as did McMaster and Mattis and Kelly. I think, in his mind, Mattis said, 'Look, as long as he doesn't go off a cliff on issues that I care about, and I'm able to influence him on the issues that I do care about, then no matter how crazy he may be on other things, because of my loyalty to what I'm doing and what I think is important, I think I need to stay here. And then I need to continue to make sure that I'm doing everything to protect not just my department or my agency, but also protect the issues that are important to this country.'"

Mattis believed in his early months on staff that he had a good relationship with Trump. He would speak with the president frequently each week, and his staff felt he had Trump's trust. Trust given not only because of his experience, but also because he did not seek the limelight, did not compete with Trump, and was very discreet about what happened in his meetings with the president. A senior NSC official said that while in their mind McMaster took a similar approach, he often "came across as too academic for Trump, too much like he was lecturing. Trump did not like to be lectured."

Christopher Ford at the beginning of the administration served on the NSC staff as senior director for weapons of mass destruction and counterproliferation. Like others on that team with whom I spoke, he had a great deal of respect for McMaster:

"H. R. McMaster, who was a very level head and a really good chap, did his hardest to insulate the NSC process, which is essential to coordinating government policy, from the challenge of dealing with the Oval [Office]. Strangely, although I was an NSC senior director and technically was a special assistant to the president, I never met Trump. I think, but don't know, that H.R. kind of insulated some of us from him, or at least those of us who were perhaps more likely than the average MAGA appointee to rub him in the wrong way. At first, as a longtime policy professional, I sort of resented that. White House jobs, after all, revolve around face time and access to the president and that kind of thing. From a traditional political and bureaucratic politics perspective, you normally don't want to be insulated from the big boss; people compete for proximity.

"But as time went by in that particular White House, I began to realize that, no, that was actually probably pretty wise, good for all concerned. It made sense to let H.R. do the heavy lifting of dealing with the idiosyncrasies of our president. And while the administration badly needed conservatives who were technocratic experts, Trump didn't always trust folks with government experience. So I ended up being happy enough working entirely through H.R. as we tried to make the machinery run as smoothly as possible, in support of the administration's agenda.

"It was a big step up from the Flynn period. To be fair, the Flynn period wasn't quite as shocking as one might have thought from mainstream press coverage at the time, and the first days and weeks of arriving in the White House are inherently sort of a frenzy anyway. And Mike [Flynn] hadn't yet gone down some of the road he has since traveled, so there was then still at least something left of the successful counterterrorist intelligence community leader to work with. So things weren't quite as nuts as a lot of journalists would have you believe. But it was a strange time, with—let's be honest—a very wide range of people. Sure, some were less serious and credible than others, but we also had folks like Fiona [Hill] and Matt [Pottinger] who were solid conservatives who were there to do the right thing; thoughtful, serious, and doing a hell of a lot of good. I won't say that there were none of our colleagues who were batshit crazy. But for the most part it was a pretty solid group, and the country is better for them having been there."

Ford, like Hill, credits McMaster with trying to get the process to run in a disciplined way, akin to how it was managed in past administrations. For example, he noted: "There was a point at which, after McMaster came in, he asked us for a couple of pages on what we saw, from the perspective of each of our directorates at the NSC, as being the greatest national security threats to the country. He wanted to orient himself, and get a feel for what his new staff was thinking. He was a very smart guy, a soldier-scholar, but it's a staggeringly huge portfolio and it made sense to survey what we were all dealing with.

"So, he wanted to get oriented, and we all submitted our 'greatest threat' lists, and one of my NSC staff colleagues wrote that the number one national security threat facing the country was from Obama holdovers. I mean, let's put this in context. At that time, Russia was building insane strategic nuclear weaponry, butchering folks in Syria, and had already started nibbling away at its neighbors and posturing against NATO. Iran was biding its time for the JCPOA [Joint Comprehensive

Plan of Action] nuclear restrictions to sunset so it could position itself on the edge of nuclear weaponization. North Korea was cranking out nuclear weapons and missiles like crazy. ISIS was still a huge problem. And China was building itself up to dominate the Indo-Pacific and overawe the rest of the world.

"But this one NSC senior staffer felt that it was the career US government civil servants who had been seconded to the NSC and were working on McMaster's own NSC staff who were the greatest threat to the United States! I thought that was a remarkable testament to how mindlessly toxic American domestic politics had become. So I guess that shows how the range of people at NSC was huge. It was a strange time, but I want to be fair to my colleagues; a lot of the time there was much more seriousness and circumspection in the mix than you'd have thought from reading the mainstream media."

A close aide to John Kelly described his mindset: "I think most of us that went in holding our nose thought, 'Well, he'll get into the office, he'll feel the weight of it, and he'll conform.' We'll be able to say, 'Stay between these boundaries.' There was something more for Kelly. I think he hadn't probably paid too much attention to the election. When you've been surrounded your entire life by a military, which is a call of sacrifice, right? It's a call of serving others, especially in the marines. It's very much other-centric service. It is almost as if they do not have the capacity to understand the narcissist that Trump was. And so I watched him over a period of months asking himself and us, 'Why would he do that?' to where he eventually became, especially as chief of staff, just like, 'Oh, yeah, that's how he is. Okay, let's work with that.'"

Another valuable perspective on Kelly's evolving mindset came from Leon Panetta, who had served as chief of staff to

President Bill Clinton. While Panetta was defense secretary for Obama, Kelly, the marine general, had worked closely with Panetta, serving as his military aide. "John Kelly called when he became chief of staff, and said, 'What do you think?'" Panetta recounted. Panetta was direct with Kelly: "John, look, number one, it's important to have a relationship of trust with a president: that he can trust you and you can trust him. Because otherwise, it's not going to work. I mean, you can do the job. You can guide the staff. But you will not have the relationship that you need in order to be an effective chief of staff. So developing that relationship is one. Number two, you do need to establish a strong chain of command."

Kelly's efforts to establish a chain of command were frustrated by Trump's instinctive preference for chaos. Panetta also told Kelly: "'Look, in addition to that, you're going to have to represent the president, whether it's on Capitol Hill or with others. And it's really important that you kind of know what he's thinking, and become an arm of the president in trying to implement policy." Finally, he told Kelly bluntly that he had to tell the president when he was in error: "I said, 'You know, John, you did that with me when you were my military aide at the Defense Department.' I said, 'You came in, and you were willing to tell me if I was wrong. Or if a mistake had been made someplace, you were willing to say it. You've got to be able to do that. There's got to be somebody in the White House that's willing to look the president in the eye and say, 'Mr. President, you're making a mistake. You're doing the wrong thing.'" Panetta had that relationship with Clinton. He would tell him when he thought the president was wrong, and of course "he got pissed off. But in the end he realized that it was important for him to have somebody who was willing to tell him that."

Panetta also hoped that Kelly could cure Trump of his social media fixation: "I told John, 'The first thing you've got to do is take that damn tweeter and throw it out the window.'" Twitter, with its immediately gratifying ability to make anyone heard on any subject, irrespective of their knowledge or wisdom, was anathema to the considered judgment necessary for good government. Panetta straightforwardly told Kelly: "You cannot have a president of the United States tweeting all day and all night. And issuing policy statements and issuing statements on all kinds of things, and not have anybody in the White House know what the hell he's doing. You can't do that. I mean, in the very least, you need to have a process whereby you say, 'This is policy.' And if you decide on policy with the president, then you say, 'Okay, you can tweet that.' But you need to have a process here. You cannot just have a president saying whatever the hell he wants to say, anytime he wants to say it. There's no way you can have an organized White House and have a president who's doing that."

Panetta attributed Trump's love of tweeting to the fact that a Twitter relationship is simplistic, shallow, and requires no lasting engagement. You can move on at any time. It suited Trump "because Trump does not want to establish a relationship of trust with anybody, and it probably goes back to New York, and dealing with all kinds of people out there. I mean, most of the people I talked to up in New York said Trump was nobody's friend."

For Kelly the challenge was obvious. If he couldn't develop a relationship of substance with Trump, then he ran the risk he'd end up being, in Panetta's words, "a hack who basically is not going to guide the White House or help guide the president, or help work through the issues, but just simply 'Whatever the hell you want to get done, Mr. President, I'll do it.'" It was a particular danger that came with the chief of staff role, and as far as Panetta was concerned, "Mick Mulvaney and Mark Meadows, I think they became hacks. Because if you're just along for the ride, you're not really doing the job of chief of staff. You might as well basically take a Secret Service agent and make him the chief of staff. Because you're spending most of the time protecting the president, you're not really doing anything to implement good policy."

Gradually, the generals and several others, notably Secretary of State Tillerson, would communicate and share strategies for how to manage the sometimes challenging, sometimes downright irrational requests that would come out of the White House. Kori Schake described it this way: "I think what the people, particularly in the Pentagon, did was try and explain to the president and his top aides why things weren't possible. There's this beautiful saying in Portuguese. It's what the Portuguese administrators in the colonies, like Brazil, used to answer when the government in Lisbon would ask them to do something that was undoable, inappropriate: 'I obey, but I do not comply.' And that, I think, is a lot of what happened. People weren't saying, 'No, I'm not going to pull troops out of Afghanistan.' What they would say was 'If we pull troops out of Afghanistan, here are the things that are going to happen. Are you comfortable with those outcomes?' That's a lot of how Jim Mattis, for example, handled his relationship with the president."

A Legitimate Way to Avoid Catastrophe

McMaster has recounted to friends how the Pentagon refused to provide military plans for strikes on Korea that were periodically requested, especially in the "hot" period of Trump tweets about Kim Jong-un, before the bromance began. Schake, an expert in civilian-military relations and co-author with Mattis of *Warriors and Citizens: American Views of Our Military,* said she thought Mattis "handled that extraordinarily adroitly. Which is to say, 'Tell me what you want to achieve, and I will draw military plans for it, but I'm not going to present Donald Trump with five ways to attack North Korea. It's better just to present one and limit his options.' So that I think is a perfect example of the legitimate use of the distributed powers in the American government to slow something down and prevent a dangerous action, by simply using the powers extant in a bureaucracy. It's the president's and the White House's job to say, 'What are we attempting to achieve?' And then the military can develop plans to achieve it. But it was not necessary to transmit every possible way to attack North Korea into Donald Trump's White House."

Miles Taylor from DHS described the growing interdependence of the president's cabinet on one another: "I think it was pretty early on that members of the cabinet started to have that conversation with each other. And a lot of them started off with the perspective of 'I'm not here for Donald Trump. I'm here to serve you, the American people, and to keep you safe, at least in the national security cabinet.' And I can point to a specific episode, and that is the first cabinet meeting, where Trump brings in the press. I remember it vividly. I went to the White House with Kelly, sitting outside waiting for him to finish, watching it live on my phone. Trump goes around to each cabinet member, and a fair number of them are just obsequious pleasers, and saying, 'Mr. President, you're the greatest,' from HHS to ag and whoever else.

"And it was primarily the national security cabinet secretaries that did not lay the praise on Trump. Instead they said, 'Hey, Mr. President, I'm honored to be in this job and to represent the men and women of DOD, DHS, State Department, etc.' I think that's the first public moment that you start to see there's behind-the-scenes conversations. After Kelly walked out, I said to him, 'I'm really glad you said what you did.' And he said, 'I did it on purpose.' He knew that there was going to be that split-screen sort of moment of who was loving on Trump and who wasn't. And I was very proud of him for that. It's written in my journal. I remember that night going home [thinking], 'Thank God he's got this clear-eyed perspective.'"

Another senior official recalled: "It was on early calls [with members of the national security cabinet] that I think everyone kind of collectively was coming to the realization that there were holes in the ship and it was sinking, because pretty much without fail, every one of those phone calls, H.R. had something to share about the president. Not in a gossipy way. He was very careful about how we framed things, but just about where the president's head was at that would make people worry.

"I'll give you an example. Let's say one week we hop on the phone, you know, H.R. would go through five things. 'Hey, you know, president's meeting with Ambassador So-and-so this week, we've got this decision coming up at the NSC, etc. But also, got to let you guys know, he keeps bringing up NATO, and then wanting to pull out of NATO.' It would be a bomb like that. And then you have Tillerson and Mattis say, 'Well, what does his day look like today? We need to get in with him before he does something stupid.' And they would go through all of their schedules and rush to the White House and have a meeting. That happened countless times, on things like NATO, threats against foreign countries, trade agree-ments, defense agreements, you name it. Or Trump would just have a knee-jerk reaction to do something and they would respond, 'Yeah, we've got to readjust everything; he can't do that. That's crazy.'"

After half a year, however, buffeted by some White House requests that did not reflect what they considered an adequate understanding of the workings of the national security side of the US government, further action was needed. Mattis, Tiller-son, and senior Pentagon, State Department, and Intelligence Community staff (along with White House National Eco-nomic Council director and former Goldman Sachs president and COO Gary Cohn) decided it would be helpful to present Trump with what one former military officer described to me as "a course in Commander in Chief 101." Another, less kind, former White House staffer called it an exercise in "remedial presidenting."

The Pentagon conference room chosen for the meeting was a nerve center for the military planning processes of the US defense establishment. Called the "Tank" (officially, room 2E924), it was the place where the Joint Chiefs of Staff met to develop strategies and resolve differences. The meeting took place on July 20, 2017, six months to the day after Trump's inauguration.

In the weeks prior to the meeting, Trump had been on a foreign policy rampage that troubled members of his cabinet. He had withdrawn the United States from the Paris Climate Accord. He was repeatedly talking about withdrawing US forces from NATO, South Korea, Germany, and Japan. He was banging the war drums at North Korea. And he wanted to find a way to absolve Russia from any responsibility for seeking to interfere with the 2016 presidential election.

Mattis speechwriter Guy Snodgrass helped to organize the meeting, which was to feature briefings from Mattis, Tillerson, and Cohn. The head of the Joint Chiefs of Staff was to be present, as was the CIA director and the secretary of the Treasury. The White House was represented by Trump, Vice President Mike Pence, Jared Kushner, and Steve Bannon.

Snodgrass described the scene as follows: "When Trump's motorcade finally pulled up, Mattis greeted the president at his armored limo, known as the Beast, and they posed for a quick photo. Reporters shouted questions, to which the president simply replied, 'We're doing very well against ISIS. ISIS is falling fast,' before Mattis whisked him into the entryway and to the conference room."

Attending the meeting in addition to Trump were the vice president, Secretary of State Tillerson, Secretary of Defense Mattis, Joint Chiefs chairman General Joe Dunford, and the White House chief of staff, Reince Priebus. Also there were the president's son-in-law Jared Kushner and consiglieri Steve Bannon.

Observing Trump's body language, Snodgrass concluded the president's mind was already made up. "He appeared to see the entire briefing as pointless." To say the meeting was a fiasco would be an understatement. Trump was visibly uncomfortable throughout the presentations by Mattis and Tillerson. The scene is expertly depicted in the book *A Very Stable Genius* from *Washington Post* reporters Philip Rucker and Carol Leonnig. On issue after issue he would not only question the presenters, but also question the underpinnings of decades of US policy. He felt supporting our allies like South Korea or those in NATO was a waste of money. Rucker and Leonnig wrote that although Mattis patiently sought to explain the value of America's alliances (which many national security experts consider one of the country's great unique assets), he did not make progress with Trump. Bannon did not help things.

Bannon interjected. "All you guys talk about all these great things . . . I want you to name me now one country and one company that's going to have [Trump's] back."

Trump then launched into a tirade familiar to those on his national security team. He condemned the Iran nuclear deal that had been negotiated during the Obama administration. Tillerson protested but was cut off.

Trump railed that the United States should get paid in oil for its efforts in the Persian Gulf (which would be illegal). Worse, when the discussion turned to Afghanistan, Trump, egged on by Bannon—whose very presence as a purely political communications advisor was anathema to the military in the room—started to condemn the generals in the meeting for their lack of success in the long-running conflicts the US had been engaged in since the First Gulf War.

"I wouldn't go to war with you people," Trump said, according to the Rucker and Leonnig account, and later confirmed for me. "You're a bunch of dopes and babies." According to one person in the room: "You could have heard a pin drop. It was about the worst moment I had ever seen between a president and his military brass." It would deteriorate from there, of course. For example, during a visit to France to commemorate the sacrifices of American soldiers in World War II, Trump balked at a cemetery visit. "Why should I go to that cemetery?" he asked. "It's filled with losers." Later on the same trip, Trump characterized the nearly two thousand marines who died in a World War I battle as "suckers" for getting killed.

Meanwhile, at the same meeting Trump made a big pitch for a military parade like the kind he had recently seen on

Bastille Day in France. But to all present, "it was clear, he did not want to celebrate the military. He wanted the military to celebrate him."

Those present were in varying degrees of shock. But one close aide to Tillerson recalled that after the meeting the secretary of state said he was "disgusted by what" he saw. To his credit, Tillerson did not just mumble his concern under his breath. He spoke out in defense of the military. Then in the wake of the meeting, after the president had left, Tillerson uttered the line for which his tenure as secretary of state will likely be best remembered. He said of the commander in chief: "He's a fucking moron."

One of Tillerson's most senior State Department colleagues told me: "I think that if there is a moment that you can identify [when Tillerson and Trump revealed their character], it is in the Tank at the Pentagon, where he and Mattis and others have hatched this plan, that they're going to bring Trump over to the Pentagon, sit him in this super-secret briefing room, and that all of the different combatant commanders are going to brief the president on US security, structure, presence, interests all around the world. And that the president is going to come out somehow enlightened. But instead of coming out enlightened, he comes out horrified at just where Americans are, and what they're doing all around the world. He doesn't understand what an aircraft battle group is. He doesn't understand what it means for the United States to send a fleet into the Mediterranean or into the North Pacific. He doesn't understand military structure and purpose. He doesn't understand duty and service to country in this regard. And he ends up kind of loudly proclaiming that everybody in the room is nuts, that the United States and his government, his presidency is way overstretched and overcommitted. But then on top of that, he criticizes the generals for not knowing how to fight wars, calling them all a bunch of losers and suckers.

"And this is where Tillerson stands up in the midst of the meeting, turns his back on the president, and tells all the military officers there that his father had been in the armed forces, and he had an extraordinary respect for them and all that they've accomplished over time. And I think that was a moment in which it obviously brewed, for him to come to this point. But what's striking is that he did it and Mattis didn't. Mattis chose not to confront the president in that moment, but Tillerson did. By turning his back on the president, by kind of reaching out to the military people in the room and expressing a sympathy and a camaraderie that the president wasn't. I think that was probably Trump's first realization, if a penny dropped for Trump, that Tillerson might not be the guy."

The official, a very experienced, high-ranking career Foreign Service Officer, continued: "People like Mattis and others realized that this was a man who knew very little about foreign affairs, about American foreign policy, and about all of the structures—the diplomatic intelligence, military law enforcement—the United States had built over years to manage a global relationship or a global presence. And that therefore there was a need to educate him. And so I think that meeting at the Defense Department at the Pentagon was designed as part of that education process, with the hope being that once he'd been educated, he would somehow be easier to manage."

"[Tillerson] said something that was quite remarkable," said Tom Shannon, who served as deputy secretary of state until May 2017. "He said when the president called him and offered him the job, he thought he had a good idea of what God had planned for him. But that as he got into the job and began doing it, he realized he was wrong. And that God's plan was not for him to do good things. God's plan was for him to keep bad things from happening." For his brief tenure as secretary of state, which could not be considered a success by any metric, Tillerson did use his stature and what one colleague of his described as his "lack of fear of Trump" to resist policies he felt were dangerous or wrong.

While other such attempts to educate and thereby manage Trump occurred, frustrations grew for each of his generals. The same month as the meeting in the Tank, H. R. McMcaster was quoted as calling Trump a "dope," a charge he later denied. In February of 2018, McMaster crossed one of Trump's "red lines" by saying it was "incontrovertible" that Russia had interfered in the 2016 elections. He resigned the following month, a week after reports began to circulate that Trump was going to fire him.

Kelly began his tumultuous tenure as White House chief of staff a week after the meeting in the Tank. It was challenging from the start, and within a year he was quoted as saying the White House was a "miserable" place to work. By speaking his mind to Trump he, naturally, alienated his boss. By December 2018, it was reported he was no longer speaking to the president. That was his last month in the White House. That same month was to mark the end of Mattis's tenure as secretary of defense. He left because Trump had on December 19, 2018, announced the United States would withdraw from Syria.

Trump had been pressing to get out of Syria for a long time. But Mattis and Joint Chiefs of Staff chairman Dunford and the rest of the top military brass, with some support from the State Department, pushed back. They felt Trump did not understand the situation on the ground and found ways to "manage" their boss—to obey without complying. In other words, they worked together to create "guardrails" against an impulsive policy decision from the president.

One former top national security official described the situation this way: "I really saw the whole guardrail thing dramatically toward the end of Mattis. It's during the second set of chemical attacks in Syria. President Trump launches cruise missiles, they destroy a couple buildings in Damascus linked to the chemical program. And everybody cheers because it shows that the United States is back in the game, and that red lines can't be crossed. And a year later Assad does it again. And [John] Bolton has just come on as National Security Council direct advisor. When the president finds out about this, of course he takes this stuff seriously first, because it's considered that Assad doesn't respect him, that Assad has decided he can get away with this. And so the president decides he needs to respond forcefully.

"But, also, the president is prone to a certain kind of odd sentimentality. If you share with him photographs of children who have been killed by chemical weapons, or women who are in the process of frothing at the mouth and writhing and dying, he gets really upset. And he wants to take immediate and dramatic action to bring down the hammer of God on the people who did this kind of stuff. And so his orders and commands were to Mattis and to Jim Dunford to prepare for a strike.

"Mattis was a remarkable guy in many ways, and a pretty tough guy. But in a couple of instances, as he dealt with these instructions he was afraid of the unintended consequences of either a cruise missile or an aircraft strike. Bolton and others convinced the president that these were what needed to be done—to not just go after Assad personally, but also to target the ground commanders that had ordered the chemical strike and those who had provided the strike, and that they needed also to go after Assad's enablers. That meant the Russians and the Iranians. And what they wanted was a very thorough, even fulsome response, and Mattis was, reasonably in my view, worried. I think Dunford also worried that if we launched a strike that killed Russians, or killed Iranians, we would be on the precipice of a larger war in the Middle East and maybe in the world."

The Time-Honored DOD Planning Dance

"So," the senior official continued, "he and Dunford went into the time-honored DOD planning dance, where they started asking for all kinds of plans to be drawn up and all kinds of target lists to be drawn up. And this just kind of stretches things out, and stretches things out, and stretches things out. So the response is not immediate. And while all this is happening, Dunford is in regular phone calls, conversations with his Russian counterpart. And this was important because it allowed the United States and Russia to have a channel of communication at a very high level, during a really delicate moment. And, anyway, by the end of the day, Bolton comes on board, and shuts down the whole interagency process, and then tries to handle the decision, basically, out of the Oval Office, but just a few people.

"And when the president finally agrees to a target package, Mattis and Dunford have reduced the targets to just a few, at an hour in which the chances of anybody being in the buildings is zero. And then afterwards we had to go and brief on the Hill, both in the Senate and the House on the strikes, and it was Mattis, Dunford, and myself. Because Tillerson wouldn't do stuff like that. I saw in Mattis a kind of real concern that the United States was edging up to a much bigger conflict, built not around a strategic assessment of what needed to be done, but a very personal impulse by the president to cause great harm as a kind of telegenic justice."

In this instance, Mattis managed to dodge a bullet in Syria. But he was unable to forestall Trump for long. For a view on that phase of the operation, I was able to speak with Jim Jeffrey. Jeffrey is a brilliant, tough-minded former army infantry officer who later rose to the highest rank in the US Foreign Service: career ambassador. Under Trump, he served as special representative for Syria engagement, and also as special presidential envoy for the Global Coalition to Counter the Islamic State of Iraq and the Levant. Jeffrey, who had served in senior positions in both the Bush and Obama administrations, does not mince words. He also holds what he characterizes as a "controversial" view that much of Trump foreign policy, such as his China policy, was successful even if some of the president's other impulses were deeply questionable. Jeffrey described the period leading up to Trump's Syria decision:

"The military, particularly [CENTCOM commander] Joe Votel, loved the counter-ISIS campaign and Syria, because it was so damn successful. For the first time, finally, we found allies [the Kurdish-led Syrian Defense Forces (SDF)] who fought like demons. They fought like the other side fought; they fought like Hezbollah. They fought like the Iranian opposition group MEK, they fought like the Quds Force, they fought like hell, they were very effective. You didn't have to worry about green on blue, all of the shit that we had in Iraq, and particularly Afghanistan. This was the opposite. These guys would go out and do their own fighting. They were first-class soldiers, and I've worked with them for two and a half years. They really are good. And it's actually the genius of their commander Mazloum. And so this was a campaign everybody loved, with low casualties. And nobody wanted to, in the military, conflate that with the awful Syria policy." The awful policy was the peremptory decision for the United States to withdraw from Syria, ceding regional superiority to Russia, with consequences that reverberate to this day.

"The first time this came up was in the spring, I think in May of 2018, where Trump decided, 'Why do I have troops in Syria? We've defeated Daesh in Raqqa.' Well, the military, aside from their cultural disposition to love this mission, also is legally bound. The only reason you have those troops in a combat zone is the 2001 authorization for the use of military force. So that they would simply say, 'We're continuing to fight Daesh,' and Trump kept saying, 'Bullshit. I've gone to the American people and told them we defeated, or Donald Trump defeated, Daesh. Why do we still have troops here? This is your own mentality to keep troops everywhere, forever.'"

According to Jeffrey: "Trump knew that we only had a couple of thousand troops in Syria and he wondered, 'If we've defeated Daesh, why can't all of our allies do this minimal role of basically training and equipping and working with the SDF, or why can't the Turks do it?' And people had to explain to him that, actually, the Turks hate the SDF whose roots are in the Turkish Kurdish separatist terrorist group the PKK. But that was his mindset. And the problem was, we kept on pushing DOD on why we were in Syria. They kept saying, 'Well, it is to defeat ISIS as per the 2001 authorization.' The

right answer was something else. And the right answer, the
first time, was 'We're there to control the terrain.' Vis-à-vis
the Iranians and Assad. And that's important for everything
we're also doing in the maximum-pressure campaign against
Iran throughout the region. That was the right answer. But it
was hard for Mike Pompeo to make that point, because they
weren't his troops. They were Mattis's troops. So we kept saying officially to Trump, 'No, they're there to fight Daesh,' and
Trump said, 'I don't want to fight Daesh anymore. I've won
the battle against Daesh.'"

Mattis's ability to manage Trump away from what he considered to be bad decisions had run out. He had fought to ensure the United States would not betray allies like the Kurds
who had fought vigorously for the US. But Trump had lost
his limited patience. Miles Taylor remembered: "I can't tell
you how many times there were conversations about POTUS
losing it and saying, 'I want to pull out of Syria.' He wanted
to pull out of Syria his first month in office, probably his first
week in office. And out of Afghanistan, and again and again
was talked into 'Hey, we need to go through a disciplined
approach here in a process to think about what the right thing
is to do.'"

Trump was talked off the ledge many times, but each time
made him more frustrated and fed up with military process. So
it wasn't out of character when in mid-December, while Miles
Taylor, John Kelly, and John Bolton were in Kelly's office, they
learned Trump had changed US policy on social media. The
president had "tweeted out that we're leaving Syria, made the
decision, immediately. You know, SecDef called. He hadn't
been consulted." Trump was "sick of all the talk" and so determined that he tweeted the decision into existence from the
residence. Mattis quit the next day.

Taylor added: "Ultimately, as those people were gotten rid of—Mattis, Kelly, Bolton, and others—[Trump] pushed forward with a 'Let's just give up on the Kurds and move on.' And a similar thing happened with Afghanistan, of course, culminating in John Bolton's departure where he was just like, 'I can't tolerate that we're having these negotiations with the Taliban and inviting them to the United States, and there's no way they're ever going to live up to these obligations. They just aren't. So let's think of a different approach.' But [US withdrawal] was pursued anyway."

When a Resignation Is an Effective Form of Resistance

In his resignation letter Mattis succinctly, respectfully, and serially went after many of the president's core beliefs, once again providing guidance and exerting a degree of pressure on Trump—pressure many thought he should have openly brought to bear earlier.

One core belief I have always held is that our strength as a nation is inextricably linked to the strength of our unique and comprehensive system of alliances and partnerships. While the US remains the indispensable nation in the free world, we cannot protect our interests or serve that role effectively without maintaining strong alliances and showing respect to those allies. Like you, I have said from the beginning that the armed forces of the United States should not be the policeman of the world. Instead, we must use all tools of American power to provide for the common defense, including providing

effective leadership to our alliances. NATO's 29 democ-
racies demonstrated that strength in their commitment
to fighting alongside us following the 9-11 attack on
America. The Defeat-ISIS coalition of 74 nations is further proof.

Similarly, I believe we must be resolute and unam-
biguous in our approach to those countries whose strategic interests are increasingly in tension with ours. It is
clear that China and Russia, for example, want to shape a
world consistent with their authoritarian model—gaining
veto authority over other nations' economic, diplomatic,
and security decisions—to promote their own interests at
the expense of their neighbors, America and our allies.
That is why we must use all the tools of American power
to provide for the common defense.

My views on treating allies with respect and also
being clear-eyed about both malign actors and strategic
competitors are strongly held and informed by over four
decades of immersion in these issues. We must do everything possible to advance an international order that
is most conducive to our security, prosperity and values,
and we are strengthened in this effort by the solidarity of
our alliances.

Even after Mattis was gone—until he reentered the public
debate as we shall see, in the wake of January 6—the views
and tactics he employed remained active. On Syria, despite
Trump's decision, the withdrawal did not take place as the
president had hoped, and the US allies in the region were not
abandoned. How did that happen? Senior planners involved
in the process recognized that the one thing Trump prized
in the region was oil. So with that in mind, they told him

troops needed to be kept in place in order to protect Syrian oilfields—in the region nearest the Kurds. Trump capitulated to this "logic," and the withdrawal Mattis felt was so dangerous was avoided.

Further, his successors learned and adopted similar tactics. Notably, Defense Secretary Mark Esper gave this account regarding being confronted by Trump's repeated demands that the United States withdraw forces from Europe: "I first meet Ric Grenell, the US ambassador to Germany, in December 2019 in London. Like Trump, he did not think Germany was a good ally. He felt they should allocate a larger share of their GDP (gross domestic product) to defense, as did I. However, he wanted to take a stick to them as the best way to change their behavior. As such, he was promoting a few ideas to achieve this end, one of which included withdrawing ten thousand US troops from Germany. I said to him, as I did to the president on a few occasions, 'I agree that Germany should pay more when it comes to their own defense. That's been the position of DOD and the White House for many years. But the way to go about it is not by using the stick and publicly humiliating them.' I told him, 'I'm undertaking a comprehensive review of US forces around the world, and the European Command [EUCOM] assessment should begin soon. I want to see the options the commander presents to improve the US presence in Europe, further reassure our allies, and better deter the Russians.' This review might just develop options that put the right type of pressure on Berlin to do more."

Esper continued: "So anyway, that was December 2019. In February 2020 Grenell returns to the United States to become the acting DNI. He and [National Security Advisor] Robert O'Brien were apparently old friends. And together, I came to learn from others, they began putting bad ideas in front of the

president. One of these directed the arbitrary and rapid reduc-
tion of ten thousand US troops from Germany, which eventually found its way into a signed presidential order in early
June 2020. I don't know exactly what provoked the action, but,
if memory serves me right, in late May [German chancellor]
Angela Merkel refused to attend the upcoming G-7 summit
in Washington that was scheduled for late June.

"At the time, Trump was trying to downplay the pandemic in the United States. So her cancellation undermined
this narrative and didn't go over well at the White House. A
few days later I received this unexpected directive, which was
rare for President Trump, to reduce the number of American
service members in Germany by ten thousand. And to make
matters worse, the president wanted to return them all to the
United States in ninety days or so. This would have been hard
on our military families, on our allies, and on NATO, and I
knew I could just not do that."

Concluding the story, Esper revealed how a potentially
catastrophic decision was thwarted. At the heart of the plan
was that the troops moved out of Germany would actually
be repositioned "forward," closer to NATO's eastern border,
closer to Russia. "At the end of the day, we developed a series
of initiatives based on five planning principles I gave the commander of US European Command, General Tod Wolters:
strengthen NATO; reassure allies; enhance the deterrence
of Russia; improve US strategic flexibility and US European
Command's operational flexibility; and finally, take care of
our service members and their families. The outcome of his
planning effort was a proposal that actually pushed US troops
further east in Europe, for example, and in ways that would
further deter Russia and reassure our frontline allies, especially Romania and Poland. General Wolters liked it because

he would have more troops forward, and we proposed other things, such as rejoining units that were geographically separated and consolidating headquarters to improve effectiveness.

"Of course, although President Trump approved our plan, the White House didn't view the broader issue the same way I did. They were more focused on taking punitive action against Merkel. I was intent on meeting or exceeding the five principles I gave EUCOM, which we did. Importantly, we convinced the president these plans would take far longer than ninety days to fully develop and implement. In my mind, I took this bowl of lemons and turned it into lemonade—into something that was really useful for the US military and beneficial to NATO. I didn't like how it all transpired at the White House. I didn't like how the president talked about it. And I didn't like how it was characterized in the media. But in the end, we produced something that met my five core principles, made strategic sense, and was far better than many imagined. If not, I was prepared to resign."

Trump was placated and the alliance was stronger. Esper and the generals had turned an effort to weaken NATO into a step that made it stronger.

The threats posed by America's forty-fifth president to the country's national security were, however, manifold. To contain them often required a whole government effort. Few areas illustrate this so well as both the visible and invisible battles over the president's approaches to America's relationships with Russia and Ukraine.

CHAPTER FOUR

Russia, Ukraine, and Constitutional Patriotism

However stupid a fool's words may be, they are
sometimes enough to confound an intelligent man.

—NIKOLAI GOGOL, *Dead Souls*

AT A FEW minutes past nine on the morning of July 25, 2019, President Donald Trump began a phone call with Ukraine's president Volodymyr Zelenskyy. He would later characterize it as a "perfect phone call."

Trump began by congratulating Zelenskyy on his party's "great victory" in that country's recent parliamentary election. "The way you came from behind, somebody who wasn't given much of a chance and you ended up winning easily. It's a fantastic achievement," said Trump.

It was clear the US president had an objective in mind when he began the call. He started by noting that "we do a lot of Ukraine. We spend a lot of effort and a lot of time. Much more than the European countries are doing, and they should be helping you more than they are. Germany does almost nothing for you." He went on to add: "When I was speaking to Angela Merkel she talks Ukraine, but she doesn't do anything." This was classic Trump on many levels. He was making the case that he was special to Zelenskyy, that he had power. And he did so in part by denigrating Germany and other European allies. He did not much like them. What he tried not to reveal to Zelenskyy was his inherent dislike for Ukraine. When he ran for president, his campaign manager had deleted from the Republican platform its statement of support for Ukraine. Trump's aides felt he just did not like the country. But, still, he wanted something from them.

His next comment revealed just what that was. It was a turning point in the Trump presidency. It would directly lead to Trump's first impeachment. Worse, within less than three years the call would help establish Trump's position as one directly antithetical to US interests—reckless and dangerous to US interests—and helpful to the interests of a declared enemy of the United States: Russia, a country with which Trump sought much warmer, closer relations.

"I would like you to do us a favor though," began Trump, "because our country has been through a lot and Ukraine knows a lot about it. I would like you to find out what happened with this whole situation with Ukraine, they say CrowdStrike . . . I guess you have one of your wealthy people . . . The server, they say Ukraine has it. There are a lot of things that went on, the whole situation. I think you're surrounding yourself with some of the same people. I would like to have the attorney general call you or your people, and I would like you to get to the bottom of it. As you saw yesterday, that whole nonsense ended with a very poor performance by a man named Robert Mueller, an incompetent performance, but they say a lot of it started with Ukraine. Whatever you can do, it's very important that you do it if that's possible."

Remarkably, Zelenskyy managed to extract what Trump was after from the mangled syntax of the president's call. The reference to CrowdStrike had to do with Trump's ongoing search for a server that allegedly contained the contents of emails belonging to his 2016 political opponent Hillary Clinton. Trump wanted assistance in tracking down the server and those who oversaw its use.

Zelenskyy agreed that he would investigate the matter. Trump then said he had heard that Ukraine "had a prosecutor who was very good and he was shut down, and that's really unfair." He said Rudy Giuliani, "a highly respected man," would call Zelenskyy "along with the attorney general." Trump then denigrated the recently removed US ambassador to Ukraine, Marie Yovanovitch, calling her "bad news." He went on to say: "The other thing . . . There's a lot of talk about [Democratic presidential candidate Joe] Biden's son, that Biden stopped the prosecution and a lot of people want to find out about that, so whatever you can do with the attorney general would be great. Biden went around bragging that he stopped the prosecution, so if you can look into it . . . It sounds horrible to me."

Zelenskyy played along and said he would look into the situation. He knew he needed the goodwill of the US president to maintain crucial support for his country. So he sought to build a bond with Trump by noting that Trump was the "first one who told me [Yovanovitch] was a bad ambassador." Trump responded: "Well, she's going to go through some things." Zelenskyy then pressed for a meeting with Trump and Trump said, "Okay, we can work that out." What Zelenskyy did not realize, but some of those listening in on the call did, was that Trump had withheld vital military aid for

Ukraine, and that he was not intending to release it unless Zelenskyy helped him dig up dirt on the man Trump felt would most likely be his opponent in the upcoming 2020 presidential election.

All such presidential calls have multiple participants listening in. On the US side, sitting downstairs in a situation room complex alongside colleagues from the NSC, the State Department, and other agencies, was Lieutenant Colonel Alexander Vindman. Ukraine, the country in which he was born, was one of his responsibilities on the NSC staff. He would later write in his book, *Here, Right Matters*, the following: "And so I did what we in the foreign-policy community so often found ourselves doing during the Trump presidency. I began to accept that all our hopes for today's chat had been dashed. I had to move on. In the face of the president's erratic behavior, that's what we'd all learned to do."

Vindman recounted that at that point he began thinking through other ways to get the ban on assistance to Ukraine lifted, knowing that if it was not lifted by early August, DOD would no longer be able to release the aid Ukraine so urgently needed. From a practical policy perspective, Vindman's focus was on freeing up the aid, but on another level the call deeply troubled him. Vindman's unease was related to the fact that Trump's focus was not on American interests; it was on his personal political agenda.

Later he told me: "There had been red flags before. I was told Trump had expressed his dislike of Ukraine multiple times, how they'd try to screw him over, that kind of stuff. We had thought we had made some progress with him in the spring of that year. But the [president] personally took whatever policy had been developed by the NSC and State and he derailed it. And it became a matter of crisis management with his tweets and everything else, and trying to get this back on track. And everyone tried to reason with him in the late spring and he's like, 'Okay, well, let's give [Zelenskyy] three months and I want to see some improvements.'" But quickly Vindman realized that a hold had been placed on security assistance to Ukraine, and it was clear the hold came from the president's team.

"We had a preparatory meeting on July 10th. Some of the president's key advisors were in this meeting, both from our team in the White House, people at State, people like [US ambassador to the EU Gordon] Sondland. And the people who were on what I call the second track of our policy with Ukraine—Sondland, [US ambassador to NATO Kurt] Volker, Giuliani track; the ones dealing via back channels with the president—they are feeding the beast, the president's known dislike of Ukraine as a way of potentially ingratiating themselves with him."

Vindman stated that "Pompeo, Esper, Bolton all tried to lift it [the hold on security assistance]." He realized the procedural problem with delivering the aid was actually coming from White House chief of staff Mick Mulvaney, who was also serving as head of the Office of Management and Budget.

Digging further, they found that the hold had been placed on the entire authorized amount of security assistance: $397 million. Bolton's team at the NSC tried to get OMB on the record about the reason for the hold, via a series of meetings in the White House. "We wanted a paper trail. Not because we thought there would be a congressional investigation, but because we wanted to make it harder for people to operate outside of channels. We also tried to keep this from becoming public because the Ukrainians were not fully aware this was going on yet," Vindman said.

Even before the July 25 call, therefore, Vindman felt compelled to report what was going on to the NSC counsel, John Eisenberg. This was toward the very end of the tenure of Vindman's then boss Fiona Hill. She had gone in to discuss the matter with John Bolton, and it was in that conversation that Bolton said, with regard to the back-channel effort to pressure the Ukrainians to do political work for the president: "Giuliani's a hand grenade that's going to blow everyone up." Hill came out of the meeting believing Bolton wanted Vindman to report what was happening to Eisenberg. But Vindman had already done that to little effect:

"I don't think [John Eisenberg] was helpful. He made the noises that he was going to be helpful. He said he would check into it. He asked probing questions like 'Is this what you really heard?' I felt like I was being managed. And that's, frankly, one of the reasons that when, after the July 25th call, I had my twin brother [the NSC's chief ethics official, Yevgeny "Eugene" Vindman] join me, because I didn't want to get into a he-said/he-said debate later on."

Making a Beeline to Legal

As a consequence of all this, as soon as Vindman heard the president ask Zelenskyy for help with digging up dirt on Biden, he knew exactly what he had to do. "I made a beeline to legal. And I went straight into my brother's office and I said, 'Eugene, if what I'm about to tell you is ever made public, Trump will be impeached.' And then I told him we had to go tell Eisenberg. I told him, 'Let's go talk to John Eisenberg,' and he was like, 'Yep, let's go.'"

In the second meeting, Vindman again felt that Eisenberg was very guarded in his response: "He's [Eisenberg] a cool customer." Vindman thought Eisenberg was understanding the significance of what he was being told, but he gave few clues. And, Vindman noticed, he took no written notes of the conversation. Vindman was glad he had brought his brother along as a witness.

Within a matter of days, what Vindman had reported started producing shockwaves across Washington, shock-waves so great that within weeks Congress was involved in the investigation that would soon turn into an impeachment inquiry. In part, this was due to Vindman's conviction and sense of right and wrong. In part, it was also due to the fact that he was not the only person who had flagged the call. While he was following procedure to report what he saw as Trump's wrongdoing, within the Intelligence Community another official was using established channels to file a whis-tleblower complaint with the Office of the Inspector General for the IC.

Michael Atkinson was the IC inspector general. He de-scribed what happened when he received the complaint: "From the moment I read the whistleblower complaint, with the extraordinary, extraordinary allegations of President Trump allegedly using his office to solicit interference in the 2020 campaign, in the election," Atkinson felt this development could have broad repercussions.

"And then [I understood] pretty quickly that the alleged phone call between President Trump and President Zelen-skyy took place the day after Robert Mueller had testified before the two House committees. Understanding that it looked like President Trump felt freed from what had been the Russia investigation. And it immediately started off with this Ukraine activity. And so that was just really astonishing to me that someone who had just put out such a huge political fire, the Russia investigation, had immediately started what I thought was likely to become another constitutional forest fire the very next day, through his call with the president of Ukraine," he said.

"I thought that the director of National Intelligence was required by statute to forward the urgent concern to Congress when I passed it along to him with my determination that it was credible," Atkinson said. "And then the Department of Justice got involved and made a determination that 'Oh, no, that urgent concern law doesn't apply' and so the director of National Intelligence has no obligation to forward the complaint to Congress. And so that was very surprising to me that what I thought was clear in the law, the Department of Justice had undone. I felt the whistleblower had pulled the fire alarm that Congress had made available to whistleblowers, and that I found the fire alarm to be a credible threat, notified the director of National Intelligence that the fire alarm had been pulled. And then, secretly, the Department of Justice came in and disabled the fire alarm so that Congress could not be alerted to what I consider to be a serious and credible national security threat."

However, Congress provides the inspector general with the authority to notify Congress if there is an instance where he feels his duties are being impeded and he therefore cannot adequately perform them. Atkinson used this authority to notify Congress that an urgent concern filing existed, even if he couldn't yet tell them the specifics or why the filing wasn't being forwarded to Congress.

This way, Atkinson triggered inquiries that ultimately led to the release of the hold on Ukrainian funds, the release of details about the president's call to Zelenskyy, and the investigation that resulted in Trump's first impeachment trial. (He is the only American president to be impeached twice during his term of office.) Reflecting back on what happened, Atkinson felt that in certain key respects "the process worked fairly well," which was generous of him since it cost him and Yevgeny Vindman their jobs. Both were fired for doing their duty, for their singular refusal to ignore presidential wrongdoing.

Whistleblower lawyer Mark Zaid reflected on what transpired: "What we often saw in the whistleblower cases is a very good example of how this system can work well, even if it faces efforts to pervert it along the way. When the complaint was filed properly through the IG system, and the IG ruled that it was an urgent concern and credible, it then goes to, in [the Ukraine] case, the direct acting director of National Intelligence, [Joseph] McGuire. And then, the law requires 'the complaint shall be transmitted to the congressional intelligence committees.' McGuire had no discretion to make that decision not to do so."

He added that in his view: "McGuire is not a bad guy in this story. McGuire was just kind of trying to figure out how best to act in an acting position while he's being told by the White House and the Justice Department not to transmit the information. But what Trump always tried to do was exploit the loopholes. Fortunately most of the time, as in this case, those loopholes were then filled in by career government officials who are in the steady state to make sure that nothing really bad happened, or at least it only happened temporarily. So, they are the guardrails. And the guardrails were steel or rubber dependent on the character and integrity of the person filing the complaint and those handling the process."

A Pattern of Behavior toward Russia

For Trump and his followers, it became an article of faith that any accusations made suggesting Trump was guilty of collusion with Russia, or showing favoritism to Russia, or doing Vladimir Putin's bidding were all part of a left-wing conspiracy they called the "Russia hoax." Of course the hoax was itself a hoax, a disinformation campaign designed to provide cover for the president's long history of dubious relations with Russia and of pursuing policies favorable to it. Or, as in the case of the Ukraine scandal, policies that might harm Russia's adversaries, like the democratically elected government of Ukraine.

Trump's withholding of funds to Ukraine and his closeness to Putin have been seen in a different light in the wake of Russia's unprovoked and unjustifiable invasion of Ukraine on February 24, 2022. Indeed, Russia's actions and their consequent implications for Ukraine, NATO, and the United States have cast a great deal of Trump's behavior in a very different light from how it was seen during his term of office—an even more damaging and disturbing light, hard as that is to believe.

Trump actively wanted to pull the United States out of NATO. He actively attacked the alliance. He advocated for a plan to pull US troops out of Europe. He advanced plans to pull US troops out of Asia, the Pacific, and the Middle East.

He effectively sought to hand Syria to the control of Russia and Russia's allies. He pulled out of arms deals that constrained the Russians. He pulled out of a deal that constrained Iran, a key ally of Russia.

He pulled out of multiple international organizations, and sought actively to weaken the international order created to contain our enemies and promote the rule of law internationally. And he tried to block aid to Ukraine.

He pushed to stop holding Russia accountable for 2016 election interference. He made it so hard for his staff to raise issues regarding being tough on Russia that they regularly simply by-passed him. And when they did take a tough stance, there was often hell to pay with the boss.

He celebrated Putin publicly and privately. Trump also regularly adopted positions closer to Kremlin talking points than to US policy. For example, from the presidential campaign onward, he would argue that the people of Crimea "wanted" to become part of Russia, downplaying Russia's illegal seizure of that territory.

Even if you did not know that Putin actively tried to help him be elected (as the intel community unanimously concluded), even if he did not surround himself with pro-Putin lackeys (as he did), even if his businesses were not swimming in Russian money, even if he did not try to block measures to make it harder for the US government to stop Russian interference in 2018 and 2020, the record is clear and shocking.

The pattern is undeniable. The consequences had he succeeded in pushing through his agenda and some of his wild ideas would have been disastrous for the United States and spectacular for Vladimir Putin. And all this was before Trump tried to blow up the very foundations of America's system and its strength with his refusal to accept Biden's victory in 2020.

If you look at not just what Trump did but what he tried to do—before he was stopped by good patriotic Americans, including many whom he had appointed to high positions— you can see that Trump's core and primary occupation when it came to foreign policy was to weaken the United States, to weaken our alliances, to weaken the international system, and to strengthen and often defend Russia's position.

Every official in the government was faced with the challenge of working with Trump on Russia-related issues. Each had to get their bearing on the president and his motives. Then each had to find a way to work with that reality even when, as often happened, what the president sought was irrational or contrary to US national interests.

General Clapper, as director of National Intelligence, was, of course, exposed to the Trump-Russia issue before the election. He observed: "We gained more insight and understanding about the magnitude, scope, depth, and aggressiveness of what the Russians were doing, and that they favored Trump and disfavored Clinton. And then we saw that their support for him was being reciprocated by Trump. That was even more concerning. So we were asking ourselves, 'What's going on here? What's up with Trump and Russia? Why's he being so solicitous of Putin and Russia?' So there were all kinds of concerns by many people about not only Trump's character, but was he compromised somehow by the Russians. I still wonder about that."

Clapper substantiates this view with the fact that senior people around Trump—ranging from those widely regarded as dependably independent-minded like Clapper's successor as DNI, Dan Coats, or those who would often waffle to appease their boss, like Mike Pompeo—all concurred with the IC conclusion that the Russians intervened in 2016 to help Trump. "He [Pompeo] did affirm, as did Dan Coats," said Clapper, "the findings of the intelligence committee assessment about the Russian meddling, and that Russians favored Trump and disfavored Clinton. And he reaffirmed that even in the face of some ridiculous posts, even critiques by his Republican colleagues on the HPSCI [House Permanent Select Committee on Intelligence]. They, in some cases, just made stuff up. So he, to his credit, when he was provided the evidence—which was pretty damn substantial, in which we had very high confidence—he publicly affirmed them, as did Dan Coats."

Clapper also took pains to point out that one point of attack against the Trump-Russia claims by Trump supporters, the Steele dossier, was not well understood. "Here's the point that people miss about the dossier," he said. "I've been bad-mouthed for the way we handled it. The FBI regarded Steele as a credible source; he'd been a professional career intelligence officer with MI-6, and was an expert on Russia. And they'd been using him for the three years after he retired. So, they considered him credible. The FBI wanted us to use the dossier as a prime source of our Intelligence Community assessment [ICA], and we didn't do that. There was a good bit of back-and-forth between mainly Andy McCabe who was FBI deputy director and my deputy Stephanie O'Sullivan. The compromise we hit on was that there were to be three versions of the ICA. In the most highly classified version we included a one-and-three-quarter-page summary description of the dossier [which omitted any of the salacious allegations] in an annex to the ICA, and explained why it wasn't used in the main body of the assessment—we couldn't corroborate the second- and third-order assets that Steele had apparently drawn on as sources for the dossier. DNI Ratcliffe did us a favor I thought, by later releasing to the public a redacted version of that annex.

"Earlier, on January 6th, after the four directors briefed the president-elect, Jim Comey briefed him alone about the existence of the dossier and what was in it. I agreed with Jim that we owed it to the president-elect to warn him about it, since it was a question of time before it came out [that turned out to be prescient, since it was released the following Monday, the ninth of January]. We also wanted to use it as an example of what the Russians might do to generate kompromat [compromising material], whether it was valid or not. You can imagine the bad tweets we'd get later, if we hadn't told him about it and he found out we'd had it, but didn't tell him about it. So, we were in somewhat of a 'damned if we do, damned if we don't situation,' but we felt that the president-elect needed to know about the dossier."

Fiona Hill, although very outspoken that she did not think Trump was an agent of Russia, did feel he was easily manipulated by Putin and the Russians: "Dan Coats [director of National Intelligence for most of Trump's term in office] expressed this in his interview with [the *Washington Post*'s Bob] Woodward that the Russians were basically trying to manipulate Trump, and there was a concern that he might give away the farm. People like Rex Tillerson, who had been dealing with the Russians for years, were very reluctant to let the president get anywhere near the [Russians]. So, we tried to find a way we could work, in some way, with his desire, for example, to have an arms control deal, while still kind of keeping his other impulses [for cozying up to Putin] under control, managing how he got information, and how choices were presented to him [trying to minimize "stray voltage" from all his hangers-on and his preferred media commentators]. The strategy, honestly, was quite sensible, but it required collective action. And that became impossible because Trump was always pitting everybody against each other. And there were so many fears, not unreasonable fears, that Trump wasn't really capable of pulling this off [effectively managing the volatile relationship with Putin and Russia]."

A key related problem with Trump, in Hill's eyes, was that "you couldn't get the guy to follow through on anything, basically. He was completely and utterly undisciplined. He did not seem to know that you can't just treat every foreign leader like your buddy. I mean, he really hadn't modified his ways of interacting with people beyond how he would have done in a business setting, which is all the glad-handing, the casual bonhomie, slapping them all on the back, bringing them into his confidence, telling them all kinds of things you wouldn't normally tell a foreign leader and certainly not an adversary. He had no filter. And that was essentially what was going on in that meeting [with Russian foreign minister Sergey Lavrov during which Trump smiled for the cameras and seemingly revealed classified intelligence]."

Jim Jeffrey attributed some of Trump's thinking on Russia to Kissinger. He said: "He is pro-Putin, and to a larger degree his pro-Putin orientation had two sources. One is, and I believe he got this from Kissinger, this idea that 'Tell me, how are you going to balance China? If Russia is its strongest ally and can provide those things, the very things China doesn't have, which is certain natural resources, oil and gas, and a lot of other things.' It just doesn't compute. But then the other thing is, Trump truly thought that his election in 2016, that the Russian thing was just an excuse for the Dems rejecting him as a legitimate president. And, of course, I don't think that's true."

Fiona Hill noted that Trump was not always undisciplined: "In the meeting in Helsinki behind the scenes he didn't behave in the same way as he later did in public. It was the press conference, that was the problem. There were times in meetings like this where he actually could be on a message to a degree, not that he ever properly prepared with his talking points. He wasn't always quite as freewheeling as he was in those early days in 2017, where he seemed to throw caution to the wind and just be excited about meeting all of these leaders for the first time, as if they were one of the CEOs he worked with in business or a fellow celebrity.

"By the time of Helsinki in 2018, he was trying to be more serious about getting arms control negotiations underway. He wanted to have business dialogue, which he and Putin had been talking about, and some of the US business community and Russian business community had also been talking about. There were actually a few modest things that he was trying to advance at Helsinki. But during the press conference it all ultimately came back to his own perceptions of what had happened in the election, and to the idea that everyone in the US press was always attacking him, and he didn't want to be humiliated in front of Putin. He basically admired Putin for being a fellow strongman, for being somebody who was running Russia like his own business, which is how he [Trump] was trying to run the United States. So what was most dangerous about him? He was just very easily manipulated by everybody.

"It wasn't that I think that the Russians especially had anything more on him than anybody else had. I mean, we all know that he was on the grift, and his business practices were deeply suspect. And all of the misogyny, sexism, all the harassment, and all the other negative things that he's done were already out there in public. The Russians probably had nothing different than all the prosecutors in New York looking into his business dealings, but he was so easy for Putin to manipulate by playing to his vanity and his insecurities.

"And so Putin would make public statements in which he would praise Trump, or he [Putin] would talk about how well the economy of the U.S was doing under Trump, knowing full well that Trump would then want to call him just to say thank you. The fact is, of course, he would never do anything for anyone other than himself. He was never doing anything for Putin. But, of course, he was useful to Putin. Indeed, we saw other people exploiting his [Trump's] vulnerabilities all the time. In addition to Russia, I had the whole portfolio of Europe. And in fact the person who often manipulated or exploited him best for their own purposes was Erdogan."

Staff and advisors would use this trait to try to "manage" Trump: "He wasn't easy to play when you actually wanted to do something positive. But he was easy to set off and to kind of manipulate into doing negative things or reacting in a negative way. So look at the way in which Lev Parnas, Igor Fruman, and Rudy Giuliani played on him to get rid of Masha Yovanovitch. All they had to do was suggest that she had dissed him, and he immediately wanted her gone. Because he's somebody who if he thinks he's lost face, and if somebody has insulted him, he wants to obliterate the person who has done that to him, even if they haven't actually done anything at all as in this case."

At the same time, because Trump was so erratic, those close to him tried to limit who ended up being exposed to him. Fiona Hill offered the example of Vindman: "Alex Vindman never even met with the president, and also after a period of time most of us didn't directly either, because they—McMaster, Bolton, and others—found [Trump] just too much of a loose cannon in meetings. It was basically like having a hand grenade with the pin off at all times. And they were extraordinarily worried about what his reactions would be to things or how he might get distracted and deliberately play to a crowd. And so they tried to minimize the number of people that came in to see him, so we would focus many of the briefings more on having the high-level intel people come in and brief him, like [Director of the CIA] Gina Haspel and others, rather than a cast of thousands from the NSC."

Miles Taylor confirmed this reality. He said: "The president never divorced the concepts of the threat from nation states to our elections, namely Russia, from the legitimacy of his own election. That's not a novel statement. I mean, I think we all know that he saw the two intertwine. But what that meant was that when the cabinet brought him options for responding to intensive Russian interest in meddling in our democracy, he was completely averse to taking action. So, anytime that we tried to brief Trump on Russia he'd be like, 'I don't want to hear it. I don't want to hear the Russia stuff, stop it with the Russia stuff!' And he would say, 'I think this is all bullshit, Intelligence Community bullshit.' I mean, he wouldn't buy it. And so it quickly became clear that those things would just need to happen below his level, of course, unless it was something that needed presidential authorization."

Christopher Ford offered a perspective on how Trump was "handled" on Russia issues and how Trump would respond. At the time, Ford was serving as assistant secretary of state for the Bureau of International Security and Nonproliferation. "I was almost fired by the president, by tweet. That had to do with the sanctions that we imposed against Russia for its March 2018 chemical weapons attack upon Sergei Skripal [the attempted murder of Sergei and Yulia Skripal, two Russian opponents of Putin] in Salisbury, England. There is a statute known as the Chemical and Biological Warfare act of 1991 that requires sanctions for countries that illegally use chemical weapons. So, after the Skripal attack in which Putin's agents used a *novichok* ["newcomer"] chemical weapon, we complied with the CBW Act sanctions rules, which was a process administered by the bureau I ran at State. My team wrote a package for sanctions on Russia for the Skripal attack, and I sent it upstairs for signature to the seventh floor, where the offices of the secretary of state and deputy secretary and other senior staff are located and it was signed."

Ford's view is that although Pompeo did not sign the document, his deputy did. And he subsequently heard that when it got to the White House, Bolton did not actually run it by Trump, presumably because of Trump's allergy to discussing anything that had to do with Russia. In any event, Ford notes, the sanctions package did move forward.

After that, Ford says: "Problem was, the president was furious that we were sanctioning Russia. I don't know if he was just taken by surprise at us sanctioning Russia, or whether he just disapproved of sanctioning Russia. But he was apparently really angry to hear about the sanctions, and was within a nanosecond of firing then deputy secretary of state John Sullivan [now US ambassador to Russia] for having signed the sanctions package. Secretary Pompeo called John and me into his office and let us have it for the trouble we'd caused with the president. I immediately offered my own resignation, if John was going to get sacked, and John and I spent the better part of the morning waiting around in his office staring at our thumbs waiting to hear whether we were going to be summarily dismissed.

"That was a bit awkward. But to Secretary Pompeo's credit—for despite the occasional haranguing, he was a great boss who supported and protected his people—he worked things out with Trump personally, to save our asses. And so I was not fired. And John Sullivan was not fired. That was my experience of almost being fired by tweet. I guess, by Trump administration standards, John and I were pretty lucky, and I'm very grateful to Secretary Pompeo for this. But those sanctions against Russia were required by law, and we were following that law."

Unraveling the Ukraine Story

In the wake of Vindman's reporting of the July 25 call to the NSC legal counsel and the transmission of the whistleblower's complaint to Congress, a congressional investigation began. This in turn led to the launch of impeachment proceedings, which in turn led to deeper revelations about the workings of Trump and his representatives, like former New York City mayor Rudolph Giuliani, behind the scenes in Ukraine.

The ability of officials to reach out to Congress as an avenue of resistance against wrongdoing is rooted in several important aspects of the federal government. One is that the employees of the executive branch also are accountable to Congress. This is an important protection against abuses from atop that branch of government. Related to this is that Congress has mandated "circuit breakers"—whistleblower laws that give officials a mechanism by which, at least in theory, they can safely challenge even those with greater statutory power or rank. Finally, there is the impeachment power granted in the Constitution as a way for Congress to hold officials accountable and to call out, investigate, and stop wrongdoing.

Trump's decision to illegally withhold congressionally authorized, much needed aid from Ukraine was an appalling act and a sign of dysfunction. But the fact that Vindman and the whistleblower were able to trigger a process leading to Trump's (first) impeachment was, in the eyes of many who participated in the process, a sign that the system was working. It signaled the successful use of constitutionally mandated channels that provide an avenue of resistance to abuses of power and perversions of the prerogatives of high office.

Rep. Jamie Raskin, a constitutional scholar, was an active participant in both impeachment processes. He agreed that the process worked to a degree, even without a resulting conviction. "There were lots of people who stood up to Donald Trump along the way," he said, "and a lot of that was about, in my mind, constitutional patriotism. Colonel Vindman is a good example. I mean, people who felt as if they swore an oath not to one guy, but they swore an oath to a system of constitutional values. And that belief in constitutional democracy itself is the sustaining ethos."

One of the values of the impeachment process was that via its investigations, closed-door and public hearings, the public came to know the full details of the president's offenses. Through the process it was made clear to everyone who watched the nationally televised hearings, or followed them in the news, that even before the July 25, 2019, phone call and its aftermath, there had been warning signals coming from the president and his political henchmen. Many abuses were enacted by the group led by the president's sometime lawyer Rudy Giuliani, and abetted by some local fixers and Trump appointees like Gordon Sondland and Kurt Volker. Among the first was the successful effort to force out the highly respected career ambassador Marie Yovanovitch, the US envoy in Kyiv, Ukraine, at the time.

For her part, Yovanovitch had been hoping for the best in her relations with the incoming Trump administration. "All of us," she told me, "were watching all of these things [the campaign], including comments, statements made during the campaign and wondering what that would mean. But I think, like many people, perhaps naively we thought that when Donald Trump became president he would adhere to the bipartisan consensus on Ukraine and Russia, and that he would learn about threats out there and everything else. And he would understand not just on Russia, but other things like NATO, etc."

Yovanovitch took the Russian threat very seriously. Speaking late in 2021 before the war on Ukraine, she said: "Russia is a historically expansionist empire. And Putin is a bully. And if we let him get away with it as we did in 2014, as we did in Georgia in 2008, as we did with Moldova, it's just going to continue." She also undertook, because it was US policy, to call out corruption and to encourage reforms from the Ukrainian government. As it happens, some of these policies put individuals close to the pro-Russian faction in Ukraine—who had been historically close to the Trump campaign—in jeopardy, and for this reason pressure grew to remove her from office.

Yovanovitch described herself as "a government bureaucrat, frankly. So I'm following what our policy is, and I'm continuing on to implement the official U.S. policy. It's not like ambassadors, or most ambassadors, have direct ties to the president and the president is saying, 'Okay, now you need to undermine Joe Biden.' That's not the way it works. So, I'm following our official policy. And, as the din got louder in late 2018, early 2019, I'm still saying, 'This is our policy.' Maybe I made mistakes along the way, but I was following our policy. And nobody ever said, 'No, no, no, we want to do something else.' Until I left."

Was she aware of what Giuliani and his associates were doing behind the scenes? "I certainly understood that there was scrutiny of what I was doing, but I didn't understand the full import of what was happening around me. And, of course, since I didn't have access to Giuliani and people like that, I didn't even know that it was coming from him. I was trained to go through official lines. In new administrations it's not unusual for ambassadors to be changed out. And so all of us were wondering if we really would be kept on." But Yovanovitch was given no indication that anything was amiss until she was summarily "yanked out of Ukraine." It was unnecessarily dramatic in some respects. "The president could have just said, 'I'm going to appoint somebody new.' And he could have said, 'We need her to leave' without the attacks on me and my reputation." But instead the impulsive president made a public show. "And people who were watching really noticed that in Ukraine and the United States."

This is echoed by those at the highest levels in the State Department. As she was being forced out and afterward, reverberations were felt throughout the Foreign Service. Career Foreign Service Officers like Michael McKinley, former ambassador to Afghanistan, Colombia, Peru, and Brazil, who was then serving as a senior advisor to Secretary of State Pompeo, were deeply concerned. In the autumn, once the rest of the Ukraine scandal came into clearer view, he brought up his concerns with Pompeo during a trip to New York:

"In my mind what was happening was beyond acceptable. And something had to be done. So I had an exchange with Pompeo which was a very short conversation. That was a very hard conversation. But he told me to drop it. And then we got back to Washington on the Saturday. I'd already decided on my course of action, and I spoke to my wife. I started a series of phone calls and emails to various people, trying to put together support inside the building at the senior level for Masha [Yovanovitch]. By the way, I hadn't talked to her. And I said to my wife, 'You know, we're going to be crossing a real line here.

And it won't be just my career in the State Department that ended badly. We could both be facing smears amd worse.' But both of us agreed that how [Yovanovitch] was being treated was unacceptable. I went through the motions (with the calls), created the paper trail with emails, and I did it very deliberately. I wasn't going to leave it at conversations on the phone that people could deny, and went on from there. What I'm describing to you is three days, four days, max four days, but I can say categorically, from the Wednesday to that Saturday, was the evolution of my reaction on the Yovanovitch issue. I thought it was an existential crisis for the Foreign Service."

McKinley resigned on October 10, 2019, in protest of Pompeo's failure to support Foreign Service Officers like Yovanovitch. A week later, he testified before the House intelligence, foreign affairs, and oversight committees with regard to his perspective on the case in the impeachment hearings.

"I think Giuliani had to establish his credibility," Yovanovitch speculated about the reasons behind the effort to remove her. "And in part, the way he established his credibility with senior Ukrainians was to move the chess pieces so that I would be removed. And he was successful." Yovanovitch suggested that "what Trump was interested in was digging up dirt on Joe Biden. But I think the other thing that he was interested in was changing the narrative. That it wasn't Russian interference in US elections; it was Ukrainian interference. And he found corrupt politicians in Ukraine that were willing to go along with that."

Yovanovitch later heard the pressure to remove her had existed for a long time, and that Pompeo had made some effort to resist it. "What they [senior state department officials] were worried about was that if I did not leave, if they couldn't report that I was out of Ukraine, Trump was going to take matters into his own hands and fire me by tweet. According to [Deputy Secretary John] Sullivan, Pompeo had been telling Trump, 'We need to keep her there.' And I guess every time Trump raised the issue his temperature was higher. The anxiety level never went back down to zero. And then finally in April, Pompeo couldn't resist anymore. I don't know if that's true. But that's the way Sullivan described it."

Yovanovitch was replaced in the job by William Taylor.

Taylor told me: "I was in Kyiv as an election observer in March of 2019, and whenever I go back, I try to sit down with whoever's the ambassador, in this case of course it's Masha. She described the things that were going on, but I still had no notion that she might be leaving or that I would ever do anything more. So in April, I guess it was of 2019, George Kent—who had been DCM [deputy chief of mission] in Ukraine under Masha and had been pulled back to the State Department to be the deputy assistant secretary for Ukraine and Moldova and Belarus and the Caucuses—called me up over at the Institute of Peace [where Taylor worked and again works as of this writing]."

According to Taylor, Kent said: "'Bill, just hypothetically, might you be interested if the opportunity arose to go back to Ukraine as chief of mission for some period of time?' And I didn't give it a whole lot of thought. I said, 'Sure, George, why not?' Within a day, I think this is right—within a short period of time, like twenty-four or forty-eight hours—I got another call from George; this was now late April. He said, 'This is not a hypothetical question anymore. Would you be willing to go back out?' And I said, 'If you're serious about this, then I need to talk to my wife, and get some other advice.' And I did talk to my wife. She didn't think this was a good idea. By this time we could tell that there was some funny business going on with Giuliani, and by this time we could see that Masha was being treated badly, and was not getting real support. So my wife had some serious concerns about this."

Taylor was not without his concerns as well, so he spoke to a number of people who could provide him with perspective on the job. These included Kurt Volker, because he was actively working on a number of related issues. Taylor continued: "I also talked to [former national security advisor] Steve Hadley. And Steve's advice is always good, solid. He said, 'Bill, if your country asks you to do something, you do it, if you can be effective.' And the last part, 'if you can be effective' was relevant in this case. Further Steve said, 'You won't know, Bill, if you can be effective unless you talk to the secretary of state to see if the secretary of state, or the State Department more broadly, or the government more broadly will support you when you go out there. Because if you're not going to get support, then you're not going to be effective.' 'But,' I said, 'I'm not really in a position to ask the secretary of state.' He said, 'Bill, if you ask for the meeting with Secretary Pompeo and he says no, that's your answer.'"

Taylor took the advice and Pompeo agreed to meet. In the meeting Taylor was direct. He said: "Mr. Secretary, your boss doesn't like Ukraine and doesn't support Ukraine. So, in that case you don't want me going out there. And, frankly, I don't want to go out there. So unless you can assure me that the US policy will continue to be to support Ukraine, I don't want to go. But even if you can give me that assurance, and if for some reason that US policy of strong support—which has been the case for decades under Republican and Democratic administrations, the House and Senate, executive branch, has supported Ukraine—if that changes, which it might under this president, then you don't want me out there. And if I were out there when that happened, I would have to come back. I would have to quit. And to my surprise, Secretary Pompeo in his office with just a couple of people around said, 'No, you're right. The president doesn't like Ukraine.'"

"And then he said, 'It's my job, me, Mike Pompeo, to turn him around. Because I'm committed that our support for Ukraine will continue. And so it's my job to get the president on board on this.' And then he said something, which was very interesting, but it wasn't quite technically correct. He said, 'Force is equal to pressure times time.' You know, this kind of physics equation. And later on I found that it was not precisely correct. But what Secretary Pompeo was trying to indicate by that statement was he was going to put pressure on the president over time to get him to change his view and to support Ukraine. And I said, 'You know, that's very encouraging to hear.'"

But then Taylor raised an issue that was troubling him. He had heard that within the State Department there was a desire to get a letter from Trump congratulating Zelenskyy on his election. But apparently the president was resisting signing the letter. Pompeo asserted he did not know about the letter. But Taylor was impressed when a day and a half later the letter was signed. This was enough for Taylor to accept the new assignment.

Taylor then described what he experienced on the job: "I encountered what I will call the 'irregular channel.' As you know, there are regular channels in every foreign policy institution. And then what I encountered was an irregular channel, which was pretty narrow and pretty thin, but pretty effective, pretty influential, and that was basically the Giuliani channel. So that's why it's irregular. I mean, he was not even a government employee, for heaven's sakes.

"The three people who had been to the Zelenskyy inauguration in May—Kurt Volker, Gordon Sondland, and [Energy]
Secretary Perry, Rick Perry—we're briefing the president afterwards in his office, telling him, 'Look, this Zelenskyy guy,
this president, he might be able to do good things for Ukraine,
and he probably is a good ally for us. We should support him.'
And Trump wasn't buying it. And they push back, I think
all three of them, but certainly Volker and Perry said to the
president, 'No, no, you're getting him wrong. You should support this.' And he wasn't buying it, and Trump said, 'Look,
just talk to Rudy.' And that established this irregular channel,
because all three of them, but in particular Volker and Sondland, at that point became part of the irregular channel. Because they said, 'Okay, boss, we'll talk to Rudy.' And they did,
which showed bad judgment, in my view. And I think Kurt
probably regretted this, but I'm prepared to believe that his
heart was in the right place. He was trying to engineer good
relations between the United States and Ukraine.

"I'd been there less than a week and a half, and there was
to be a phone call with Sondland, Volker, Perry, and Zelenskyy, and they added me to the list of participants for this
conference call. They were working out the timing of the call.
Prior to the call, Gordon Sondland called me while I was out
for a walk with my security detail, and he said, 'We're gonna
change the time of the conference call with Zelenskyy. By
two hours.' I said, 'Fine. You're going to let your staff and the
other staff know so they can make the adjustments?' And he
said, 'Well, no, my staff doesn't need to know, no staff.' But
they were not my staff, so I let it go, but a little flag went up.
Another thing about the call was weird.

"We Americans got on this phone call before they introduced President Zelenskyy to the call: a pre-call, a discussion

before Zelenskyy got on the call. Sondland wanted to be very sure, because it was the State Department ops center that was putting this call together, that no one from the ops center was going to monitor the call. He wanted to be sure that there would be no note taking, that there was nobody from the State Department or anywhere else on this call to listen to him. And the ops center said, 'Fine, we'll set it up and we'll drop off and that'll be it.'

"So that was another indication to me there was something real funny here, a little odd. Got on the call and the call was okay. And I now realize, after the fact, that what we're really trying to do was to get President Zelenskyy to commit to these investigations. But they didn't want to say it on the phone. And they certainly didn't want to say the word "Biden," didn't want to say "Burisma" [the Ukrainian company on whose board sat Biden's son Hunter] or have anyone use any of these terms. But they wanted to be very sure that on the phone call being planned with President Trump—what would be the notorious July 25 phone call—that Zelenskyy would say the right thing, because if he said the right thing, then the meeting that had been promised in that letter could take place. The meeting in the Oval Office could take place, and they could schedule it and hold it. But until Zelenskyy committed to these investigations, they weren't going to schedule the meeting."

On Direct Order of the President

In mid-July, at a regularly scheduled meeting of all the senior officials involved in Ukraine policy, in which much of the discussion was about energy, another development raised Taylor's concerns: "I could see something really bad happening at the end of that meeting, when I could see a hand go up. I couldn't see whose hand it was, but the person said, 'I'll tell you that we at OMB have been instructed by the president's chief of staff, who was instructed by the president, to suspend security assistance to Ukraine.'

"Pin drop. Total silence. Alex Vindman was caught totally by surprise. He was chairing this meeting. And Alex pushed and asked, 'What do you mean?' The person said, 'Listen, I can't tell anything more. I'm just saying that we've been told at OMB on direct order of the president through the chief of staff to us.' So that was the time that I knew this was a big problem.

"Ultimately, we came to know that the president had decided he was going to keep back the security assistance. So, they were not just going to use the meeting in the Oval Office that Zelenskyy wanted to squeeze them to do these investigations. No, that wasn't enough. He was also going to put security assistance on there as well, and use that as leverage to get them to do the investigations. We figured it out later. We didn't know, but it was stunning.

"Mark Sandy, who is as you know, a career OMB official, and he had gotten this instruction. And he resisted it for the reasons that you said: we can't do this. The monies have [been] appropriated. And it's been signed into law. It's an appropriation. But he created a mechanism, which was in the form of a footnote to the order, or to the allocation, I think it was. Again, Mark knows this stuff. I don't know this technical stuff very well—a footnote to the allocation order that says we're going to do some more checking on this assistance before we let it go. And there was a limited amount of time, because the funds already were appropriated. And so they could only pause the assistance for a limited amount of time, suspend it, or pause it, or keep it from flowing. Mark's a great guy, by the way. He's a great guy, a real patriot, real dedicated. He's the senior civil servant at OMB. Everybody above him was political. Everybody below him is professional, civil service. And so he bore that burden. He was trying to protect his people. He was trying to resist the pressure he was getting to do illegal things. And it's looking for ways to try to make this work and keep people out of trouble.

"A limited number of people were on that call [the Trump-Zelenskyy July 25 conversation], including Alex Vindman. Not including the whistleblower, not including any of us at the embassy, and not many people in the State Department. But I think Pompeo was on there a couple of minutes. But overall it was a small group. And if you talked to Alex [Vindman], that he was told to go to great lengths to put the minutes of the call in a 'lockbox,' to put it in this file that was very secure and nobody could see it. So no one knew what was in that call until it was released in September, when Zelenskyy was meeting with Trump at the UN. So this happened after the whistleblower had already blown that whistle. And Trump was trying to defuse that, and he said, 'Oh, well, it was a perfect phone call. So, we'll just release the transcript of it.' But they gave the poor Ukrainians like five minutes' notice that they were going to release this transcript. And they were horrified. The Ukrainians were displeased because Zelenskyy had had what he thought was a protected, or at least confidential, call with the president of the United States. It was in that phone call, for example, that they both bad-mouthed Masha. But President Zelenskyy had no idea this was going to be a public call. But by the end of August and beginning of September it became clear. The light finally dawned on many of us, including me, what was going on with this irregular channel. But it wasn't until the end of September that the phone call was released. And at that time it was so clear what went on.

"Tim Morrison and I had been in touch ever since he took over from Fiona [Hill, as senior director at the NSC]. He was also horrified by this interagency meeting, where the OMB person said we're going to pause this assistance. Afterwards, he and Alex had been scheduling meetings at ever higher levels. And on the agenda for each of these meetings was this pause of assistance to Ukraine caused by some misunderstanding or some garbled instructions. No one could understand why it was being held, including Tim, including me. He scheduled all these meetings where in the end Pompeo was supposed to be there with Mark Esper and Gina Haspel, who was the director of the CIA. They were all there. They were trying to get Trump to change his mind to let this assistance go. They were not able to do that, as we know, and he only changed his mind once the whistleblower blew the whistle, to let it go."

Taylor clearly had come to a turning point, the moment he had anticipated in his conversation with Pompeo. National Security Advisor Bolton was on a visit to Kyiv. After his scheduled meetings had taken place, he and Taylor had a private exchange in a secure room. Taylor recalls: "I had this very direct conversation with him [Bolton] saying, 'Look, I had this deal with Secretary Pompeo. That if the support for Ukraine changes, if we withdrew our support for Ukraine, that I would quit, and I'm about to do that.' Bolton said, 'You should write a first-person cable just to Pompeo laying out your arguments.' And that's what I did. It was a no-distribution cable just to Pompeo. At the end of the cable I said that I would quit. That was about the time my wife and family were planning two different trips to Ukraine, to visit me to see the sights of Kyiv in November and December. And about the time I was writing the cable to the secretary, I told my wife, 'I can't tell you anything, but be sure you get refundable tickets, because I might not be here by then.'"

Mark Esper had just been sworn in as secretary of defense in late July. He says he was not aware of the Ukraine issue when he took office. But almost immediately, the question of the withheld aid arose and both he and Bolton went to the president to try to convince him to release the funds. Their efforts were unsuccessful. Esper's team, including DOD comptroller Elaine McCusker, kept him informed of looming legal deadlines and made a careful record of exchanges with the White House and the rest of the administration.

Esper recalled that when he did raise the issue with the president: "He would just push back and say, 'They're corrupt. We shouldn't give corrupt governments more money.' He would add Germany and other countries close to Ukraine should be the ones giving more money.' And my response would usually be 'Yes, you're right. There is corruption in Kyiv. But the new president, Zelenskyy, is trying to change that and we need to support him.' Then I'd say, 'Number two, Mr. President, when I talk to my German counterpart at NATO, I will raise this issue and tell them, that they need to give more support to Ukraine.' And number three, I'd say to him, 'Releasing the funding is the law. We don't have a choice, when Congress appropriates it. We have an obligation to get the money out the door.' But those arguments and the others that Bolton and Pompeo might have made fell on deaf ears." Esper noted that it was not until later, after the transcript of the president's call with Zelenskyy was released, that he became aware of Trump's real reasons for blocking the aid.

Elaine McCusker recalled: "I started getting increasingly concerned about the situation with the hold-up in aid to Ukraine. I had a close partnership with my general counsel colleagues and was talking to them constantly about it. As it became later and later in the fiscal year, I didn't know how we were going to get to a decision. We were told what to do in increments. And every time we came across a deadline, we were told to hold for longer.

"I wasn't really thinking outside my own lane, my responsibilities. And I think I was doing what you would want your comptroller to do. I hope that we haven't sent a signal to the comptroller or to the general counsel not to do that. Because as a taxpayer, as a government, you need your comptroller and your general counsel to tell you the sometimes unattractive truth of things. And if they stopped doing that, that would be bad for everybody."

It was not until August 28, 2019, when Politico reported the funds were being withheld, that the issue became public knowledge. It is not clear whether prior to this Ukraine even knew there was a problem. Within days the plot thickened. On September 1, Sondland made it clear to the Ukrainians that unless they made an explicit promise to pursue the Burisma investigation—into the alleged ties between Joe Biden's son Hunter and the energy company Burisma in Ukraine—the funds would not be released. That same day, Taylor told Kent that Sondland had been as explicit in his communications with the Ukrainians as to say that Trump wanted Zelenskyy at a microphone voicing the words "investigations," "Biden," and "Clinton." The *Washington Post* would report the shakedown attempt four days later, on September 5. Still, Sondland kept pressuring the government of Ukraine. Taylor confronted Sondland, saying: "I think it's crazy to withhold security assistance for help with a political campaign."

Impeachment

The House foreign affairs, intelligence, and oversight committees announced the whistleblower complaint on September 9. Two days later, Bolton resigned. Two weeks later, Nancy Pelosi, leader of the House, called for a formal impeachment inquiry, and Trump released his transcript of his "perfect" phone call. Information about the complaint and the cover-up started to flow rapidly as Congress investigated. On September 27, Volker resigned. The next day, McKinley began his effort to seek a State Department statement defending Yovanovitch. McKinley would resign ten days later.

During the month of October, Yovanovitch, Sondland, Hill, Kent, McKinley, Taylor, and Vindman testified at the House inquiry. Mulvaney independently, explicitly said Trump was seeking a "quid pro quo"—getting a promise of investigations in exchange for the release of the military aid.

On December 18, 2019, the House voted to impeach Trump by a vote of 230–197, making him only the third president in US history to be impeached. The Senate would vote to acquit Trump by a vote of 52–48 on abuse of power charges, and by 53–47 on obstruction of Congress charges. But by then the plot to withhold funds had been revealed, the funds had been released, and the world had gotten a much closer look at how Trump operated, particularly with respect to issues associated with Russia and Ukraine, which would prove even more illuminating and disturbing in years to come.

What the public also could discern, if it listened to the testimony presented to the House, was what we have heard from
the participants. There were multiple efforts to hold Trump
to the law and to encourage him to act in the national interest, even when his impulse was to do otherwise. Trump's impulsiveness, recklessness, inexperience, narcissism, and biases
also forced senior officials to find ways to balance his demands
with the requirements of the law, regulations, and their oaths
of office.

Sometimes they were successful. Certainly they were doing their duty. In the end that did not protect their careers.
Yovanovitch, Vindman, Atkinson, and McCusker lost their
jobs as a direct result of the events described here. Taylor and
McKinley resigned rather than act contrary to the interests of
the country and the department in which they served.

Atkinson said: "I thought the protections of the independence of inspectors general did not hold up. I felt like I
got fired for being independent. Which is what the law required me to be, to be independent. To be objective. And yet
I got fired for being independent." Zaid also confirmed that
the White House made an effort to leak the whistleblower's
name, to generate negative publicity and consequences for the
whistleblower—a step completely antithetical to the spirit and
the letter of whistleblower laws.

McKinley remained angered by the human toll the process had taken. "Where was the significant effort to protect
whistleblowers? Talk to some of the people involved. Talk to
Masha. Talk to George Kent. Talk to Vindman. Talk about
the level of threats they and their families received from the
dark web and crazies, but also about the vilification coming
out of the White House. There was no great protection for

them coming out of Congress. And [Congress] did not rush forward to help us pay our legal bills, did they?"

McKinley added: "Having said that, many people in many different buildings responded and did what they had to do. I certainly consider my part a very, very small part of the story. But what Masha and George [Kent] and Bill Taylor did was significant. What Bill Taylor did was demolish any effort to present Ukraine policy as anything other than what it was. To tell the truth and let the truth be known, because he was so systematic and he kept such detailed notes. And so people like him were absolutely integral to this and to our system surviving this kind of abuse."

CHAPTER FIVE

We Have to Act
Like We're Taking
This Seriously

What public health is really is a trust. It's a trust
between the government and the people.

—**LAURIE GARRETT**, *Betrayal of Trust*

THE COVID PANDEMIC is the worst public health
crisis in US history. During the 1918 flu pandemic,
whose worldwide toll included 50 million deaths and
resulted in 500 million people being infected, 675,000 Americans died. In early 2022, the US official COVID death toll
passed one million. According to experts, the real toll is at
least 20 percent higher, due to undercounting or cause-of-
death misclassifications.

In 1918 the United States, thanks to comparatively swift
enactment of sound public health policies, saw a lower in-
fection and mortality rate than most nations worldwide. But

through early 2022, the US had the highest mortality rate from COVID of any developed nation. This was at least 63 percent higher than that of any other wealthy nation, according to a *New York Times* study. At the time of the study, 36 percent of Americans were not fully vaccinated, a higher percentage than in any of the other ten high-income countries to which the United States was compared.

There are several reasons for this, according to experts. One is that the United States lagged in its responses to the virus, from testing and tracking to implementing measures— such as mask mandates, social distancing, lockdowns, and, later, vaccines—to protect society. Another is that pandemic-related issues ultimately became politicized. By 2022, when most deaths due to the virus were among the unvaccinated, "red" counties, those that in 2020 voted for Donald Trump to become president, had a death rate three times higher than counties that voted for Joe Biden.

According to a commission created by the respected medical journal the *Lancet*, poor policy choices made in 2020 by the Trump administration, when the virus broke out, may have been responsible for 40 percent of virus-related deaths during Trump's term in office. In the words of the commission's report, which condemned Trump's response to the pandemic, America's forty-fifth president "brought misfortune to the US and the planet."

In an op-ed in the *New York Times*, two epidemiologists, Britta L. Jewell and Nicholas P. Jewell, estimated that 90 percent of early deaths related to the disease could have been avoided had social-distancing measures been introduced just two weeks earlier. They wrote: "Whatever the final death toll is in the United States, the cost of waiting will be enormous, a tragic consequence of the exponential spread of the virus early in the epidemic."

The decision by Trump and his supporters to make wearing masks, social distancing, and getting vaccinated a fault-line political issue in the United States may have been one of the most reckless and irresponsible in the nation's history. There were approximately 400,000 officially recorded coronavirus deaths by the time Trump left office. But of the 500,000 that followed afterward, the vast majority occurred among the unvaccinated. This led to the description of this second phase of the COVID crisis as a "pandemic of choice." In excess of 90 percent of deaths due to the disease in 2021 and 2022 were among the unvaccinated; some estimates say 99 percent. Those who died were largely people who embraced the Trump-bred GOP line that doing the right thing from a public health point of view was an infringement on personal freedom. As of this writing, this point of view still predominates in red states and counties across America, and it has certainly prolonged the pandemic in those regions.

The cost of the pandemic was not, however, purely one that could be measured in infections, or even in mortality. The worst public health crisis in US history also became the worst economic crisis since the Great Depression, one made worse by the depth the crisis reached due to Trump and his team's failures in public health policymaking and implementation.

Some 40 million Americans lost their jobs as a result of the crisis. The unemployment rate reached 15 percent in April 2020. In the second quarter of 2020, US GDP contracted by 31.7 percent, by far the largest such downturn in US history. As a result of the crisis, one in five mothers of children under twelve reported their children were not getting enough to eat.

America's response to the crisis, which included, almost unbelievably, pulling out of the World Health Organization in mid-2020, caused its international standing to plummet. Under President Barack Obama, a Pew Research Center poll of thirty-two countries showed almost 75 percent of those contacted had confidence in the American president to "do the right thing." Under Trump, even before the crisis, the number was 29 percent. Even Vladimir Putin ranked higher.

In short, not only was the pandemic a catastrophe for the public, but also it reflected one of the most shocking breakdowns in public policy history, a combination of extraordinary negligence, ignorance, mismanagement, and malfeasance on the part of Trump and his team.

The objective of this book has been to provide examples of how government professionals—appointees and career officials—served as guardrails, limiting the damage Trump and his inner circle could do. Clearly, in this case almost unimaginable harm was done. As in the cases of US abuses at the border and its reckless national security policy, the harm is not to be minimized. (There are plenty of books, articles, and studies focused more specifically on what went wrong.) But even in this instance, despite the disastrous consequences of Trump's behavior and policies, it is possible to draw one conclusion. Had it not been for the dedicated effort, often in very hostile working conditions, of senior- and working-level federal government officials, the outcomes could have been much worse.

Here, of the four principle areas by which US government outcomes are influenced—process, politics, policy, and people—the character and capacity of our health care leaders mattered greatly. Especially when the president himself, and some of those around him, were as defective and dangerous as they were.

Immune to Facts or Logic

"I would brief him and his attention span was often very short," Dr. Anthony Fauci said. "You would be sitting down with him and you'd be trying to get a really important point across to him. And he'd be asking questions that are unrelated to what you're talking about. That scared me a bit. Because I'm used to dealing with life and death situations. You're in the middle of trying to make a really fine point of a subtlety of what a pandemic outbreak might mean such as why even though there were at the outset just a few cases in the United States, we have got to be really careful—and then he'd start talking about a friend of his who has a different opinion.

"I mean, if I told him that five highly respected scientists found out something that's important, you'd get the impression that when he called up his buddy from Queens, that person's opinion was equally as valid as the five scientists that I'm talking about. So right from the get-go, I got a little nervous about the relationship between what I'm doing with him and scientific reality."

Fauci had experience with every American president since Ronald Reagan. But when it came to the biggest public health crisis the country had ever faced (and of course Fauci was on point through many big crises, including AIDS), the president he had to deal with was uniquely ill qualified to comprehend the reality of the situation. One former Trump White House staffer described the president as being "immune to facts or logic. Or maybe vaccinated against them."

When in January 2020 the first reports of COVID started coming into the White House, there was a sense among public health professionals that it might be something to watch closely. Olivia Troye, who by that point was working on the vice president's national security team, and who would later be his point person on the Coronavirus Task Force he chaired, said she was among them: "I knew from day one that this was going to be really bad for us. And the scientists were concerned, that was clear."

Troye described how it impacted her personal life: "I went out and bought N-95 masks for my family in January, because I knew that they were going to disappear. When there's a snowstorm, there's a run on milk and cheese and eggs, right? So I had a fight with my husband, and I'll never forget it. When I had been asking him to stock up for the house in case we can't leave the house for thirty days. That's how I was preparing. But I am a resilient person who prepares for the worst, right? I'm not necessarily a prepper. But I'm certainly one of those people that keeps the backpack ready for a disaster. So I had a massive fight with my husband in February where he still hadn't gone to Costco to get the stuff that I told him to get. And he finally goes, and thank God he did, because he does it literally, I think, the week before we go out and tell people you need to get masked, we might be shutting down the country, and then there's a run on it."

Troye and her fellow task force members were very concerned at the rate of spread in China and massive government reaction there that included the very rapid building of new hospitals. They were certain the virus would reach the United States, partly because of the time of year. Many people had traveled internationally over the Christmas and New Year holidays. "I was like, there is no way that this thing is not here. Especially given that, by the way, we're right after the holidays. So, this thing didn't just suddenly appear in January. I don't believe that at all. I believe that it was probably sort of already there and already spreading."

Other parts of the US government also sprung into action. One example was the Department of Defense, which relished and took advantage of the fact that much of what it did was separate from what was going on in the White House, and often beneath the radar of the White House.

Secretary of Defense Mark Esper described the DOD response: "The first reported COVID case was identified in the United States on January 21st or -2nd. Several days later, on February 1, we implemented our global pandemic response plan—weeks before the first person in America actually died from the coronavirus—because we didn't know what this virus was or where it was going. Better safe than sorry. As part of our plan, DOD had stockpiled medical equipment, ventilators, masks, other PPE, and so on; all the things that HHS and others seemingly didn't have. We were relatively well prepared, though not perfect as we came to learn, and improved over time. What we also started doing was issuing medical guidance memos to the department to safeguard the health and readiness of the force. In fact, I issued the first one on January 31, with a dozen or so to follow over the succeeding months. My messages often repeated my three priorities: protecting our troops, DOD civilians and their families; safeguarding our national security capabilities; and supporting the president's whole-of-nation response. The early and continued issuance of guidance memos to the department proved vital to our success, punctuated by the fact that we only lost one active-duty service member to COVID during my tenure. In early April, the CDC [Centers for Disease Control and Prevention] issued guidance that everyone should wear masks. Within two days, we had everyone in DOD masked up—the first department to do so. This stood in stark contrast to the White House, which I don't think ever really did."

"So in April, we're social distancing, we're wiping down furniture, and we're masking up at the Pentagon," Esper continued. "And these types of actions we are taking increasingly diverge over time with the White House and what the president is saying. While Trump is declaring that COVID will soon disappear, I was talking to the force about this pandemic lasting into the fall. But one of my biggest concerns came in the summer of 2020, when the White House began talking more about reopening the nation's schools in the fall. The Defense Department has 160-some schools spread around the states and globally, so I had to figure out how best to approach the issue. One thing was clear, however: we couldn't risk the safety of the children. And so I decided we weren't going to just automatically open the schools. Rather, we took a tailored approach that was conditions based and considered a variety of factors on a school-by-school basis, allowing local commanders to make the call that was best for their community. It was clear, though, that this was another area where we were clearly diverging from the White House."

There were also some other people who were, like Troye on the White House staff, more concerned earlier than most. She gave an example: "Strangely, given the other issues with him, Peter Navarro, who was a trade guy, he got very engaged."

According to a senior trade official who worked with Navarro at the time: "That was because the origin of the disease was in China. Peter hated China. Pathologically. And he saw this as an opportunity to set in motion some of his most extreme policies to block trade with China, in much the same way that Stephen Miller and the immigration hard-liners would later see it as a way to shut down the southern border. That was telling. Political opportunists around the president did not see the disease for the threat it was. They saw it for what they wanted it to be, something that would serve their agendas." Olivia Troye confirmed this view, stating: "Navarro was very concerned. He was concerned about PPE [personal protective equipment] and supply chains. And I think he was concerned because the virus came from China and he's a China hawk."

Having such a wild voice as Navarro's intervene on COVID was not especially constructive, even if his alarmism was well founded. The problem was that he was so unreliable and outside the mainstream on most issues. One senior official who was in most of the high-level COVID-crisis Trump administration meetings summed up Navarro as "a fucking sociopath." (His subsequent role as a cheerleader for the Big Lie made this clear to many Americans, but it was a fact known to many who had dealt with him as a "trade" or "China" expert in the years before he joined the administration. As an editor who saw his work during those years, I think it is fair to say he was pretty widely viewed as a crackpot.)

Team Trump did not just contain key players ill-suited to handling a crisis like the coronavirus pandemic. They had also made it harder for the rest of the administration to handle it. In 2018, Trump's White House staff had disbanded the White House pandemic response team. Effectively, they tossed in the waste bin the plan the Obama administration had put in place to deal with such situations, following the Ebola outbreak they had confronted. Later, when the Centers for Disease Control and Prevention epidemiologist assigned to work within China's CDC counterpart left his job, the Trump administration eliminated the position.

Trump's bravura and ignorance led to his assessment on January 22, 2020, that the United States was on top of the potential threat caused by the new virus: "We have it totally under control. It's one person coming in from China. It's going to be just fine." Two days later, Trump praised China's President Xi for his handling of the crisis, saying: "China has been working very hard to contain the coronavirus. The United States greatly appreciates their efforts and transparency. It will all work out well. On behalf of the American people, I want to thank President Xi."

Behind the scenes, Trump was getting reports that matters might be more serious than he was willing to let on publicly. On January 28, his national security advisor Robert O'Brien, a lawyer not known for rocking Trump's boat, told the president: "This will be the biggest national security threat you face in your presidency. This is going to be the roughest thing you face." Two days later, a Navarro memo to the president read: "The lack of immune protection or an existing cure or vaccine would leave Americans defenseless in the case of a full-blown coronavirus outbreak on US soil. This lack of protection elevates the risk of coronavirus evolving into a full-blown pandemic, imperiling the lives of millions of Americans." (Proving that even "fucking sociopaths" are on occasion correct.)

Behind the scenes, Troye wrote a memo that passed up through her boss General Keith Kellogg, national security advisor to the vice president, saying that the United States should ban foreign nationals entering the US from China. She felt that both Pence's chief of staff Marc Short and Trump's chief of staff Mark Meadows "thought I was nuts."

Kellogg in this instance had Troye's back. When she later became a prominent Trump critic, he changed his tune. But according to Troye, Kellogg defended her robustly at the outbreak of the pandemic, saying: "She doesn't spin things. She is very factual and very thorough in her approach. And so if she's saying that this is going to happen, the likelihood that it's going to happen is probably like 99 percent that's going to happen." According to Troye, the VP and his chief of staff were shocked at her conclusions and the forcefulness of her warnings. "Marc [Short]," she noted, "couldn't be bothered with it. Neither could Mark Meadows. This was like the worst thing to them. This was a distraction. That was a pain in their ass. And this was the last thing they wanted to talk about. [Marc Short] laughed in my face when I told him we were going to ban travel from China."

Trump continued to downplay the threat in public, beginning the pattern of acting according to how he felt the virus reflected on him personally or politically, ahead of reality or the interests of the American people. On February 2, Trump would say: "We pretty much shut it down coming in from China." Five days later, speaking during a phone call to Bob Woodward (as Woodward would later recount) he observed: "It's also more deadly than even your strenuous flu. This is deadly stuff." A couple days later he said: "Looks like by April, you know when in theory it gets a little warmer, it miraculously goes away." Two weeks after that he boasted: "The coronavirus is very much under control in the USA. The stock market is starting to look very good to me." On February 25, he congratulated his own administration for doing a great job on COVID. The same day he said: "We're very close to a vaccine." The first vaccines in fact appeared many months from then. He called the coronavirus outbreak a "very little problem" the next day. The day after that he said: "It's going to disappear. One day, like a miracle, it will disappear." In February 2020, almost all the president's public comments on the coronavirus were meaningless bluster, a showman's attempts at distraction.

Meanwhile, behind-the-scenes alarms were sounding. Fauci and the task force initially assigned to track the threat—led by Health and Human Services (HHS) secretary Alex Azar plus doctors from CDC—were concerned. They were seeing signs of international transmission. But, still, there were only a handful of cases in the United States. So Trump kept on downplaying the threat. And he was pressuring CDC to do the same.

During a now infamous visit to CDC in early March 2020, Trump once again tried to play down the threat posed by the disease, while at the same time attempting to show he was completely on top of handling the response to it. In answer to criticism that the United States had not sufficiently ramped up its COVID testing capacity he said: "Anybody right now, and yesterday, anybody that needs a test gets a test. They're there. And the tests are beautiful. The tests are perfect, like the letter was perfect. The [call with Zelenskyy] transcription was perfect. Right? This was not as perfect as that but pretty good." He then added: "I like this stuff. I really get it. People are surprised that I understand it. Every one of these doctors said, 'How do you know so much about this?' Maybe I have natural ability. Maybe I should have done that instead of running for president." He also stood by a decision not to let a cruise ship with infected passengers on board dock in San Diego because "I don't need to have the numbers double because of one ship that was not our fault."

One member of the White House task Force team said: "I was horrified by what he said during the CDC visit. Also, it was exactly what I was expecting because I've seen this Trump show over and over again. And I was like, he's gonna make a mockery. And those people are in the fight of their lives right now, right? It's not gonna help the situation."

The capitulation to pressure of the CDC team and its head, Dr. Robert Redfield, was yet another sign of problems to those in the White House working on the situation. One senior medical member of the team said to me: "Bob Redfield was a disaster. He was a total disaster. He allowed the CDC to be overrun by the politicals. There were people telling the CDC what to write. And he should have fallen on his sword, right there, in Times Square, at high noon. And he didn't. So that was bad."

Perhaps because of the dysfunction within the task force team, or perhaps because Trump really felt the COVID outbreak was an insignificant distraction that would disappear of its own accord, in late February the vice president was put in charge of it. Troye recounts: "I knew this was going to be very bad for us [the country] when in an early meeting, I was there in the room when somebody said, 'We have to act like we're taking this seriously.' I'll never forget that statement for the rest of my life. Because I walked out of that briefing thinking, 'No, we don't have to act like we're taking this seriously. We need to be actually doing something right now.'"

Troye felt Pence added a stabilizing influence to the process, even if he was not known for challenging the president. "Pence is factual. And from the beginning he was factually briefing people with what was really happening. At the outset, I don't think he was deeply engaged. That was frustrating for me. I felt that in his office, for a while there, I was on my own island. The reality is, I struggle with Pence. He did [take it seriously]. I mean, once he took over the task force he realized that he owns this thing. And then once he starts to get briefed, and he's in these meetings, and he's running it, and then he starts to talk to the governors. And I think that's what actually shakes Pence—he's a former governor."

Pence started to place a series of calls to governors across the country, in red and blue states, and Troye sat in on many of them. She felt the vice president's mind and mood change as he started to hear from those on the ground, at the leading edge of the COVID outbreak: "He starts to internalize this and realize this is very real, people are in a really bad situation out there." Sometimes in a broken-process environment like the Trump White House, maintaining active contact with the outside world, with a different perspective, with the situation on the ground can be a vital antidote.

By March 11, the World Health Organization had categorized the disease as a pandemic, due to the speed with which it spread and the severity with which it hit patients. The task force recognized something different and drastic needed to be done, and they needed to find a way to sell it to the president.

Pandemic and Infodemic

"I can best describe the task force by comparing it, in some respects, with what we have now with the [Biden administration] medical team in the White House," said Fauci, providing an overview of the process operating in the White House during early to mid-2020. "At the moment, we really have a structure and an organization with a plan of how we're going to address the outbreak, how we're going to end it, how we're going to mitigate it, how we're going to do all those things. And it's a group that essentially meets and talks every day, multiple times a day. With the Trump task force, although there were good people on the task force, there was a feeling coming from above almost like, 'I wish this damn outbreak would go away. We want to get on to saving the economy.' The only reason why they were intensifying their focus on it was the impact on the economy.

"So, the task force was heavily dependent on [White House coronavirus coordinator] Deb Birx, who was one person who got all the data and knew everything that was going on; the vice president is a good man, whose heart was in the right place, but was so fiercely loyal and unwilling to conflict with the president. He never challenged President Trump and said, 'No, what are you doing?' It was always 'How do we get our job done without getting him upset?' And to his credit, the vice president was trying to make things work, often saying, 'Tony [Fauci], what do we need to do? Deb, what do we need to do?' And then he would try to figure it out, try to work out how we could present it in a way that would be compatible with what the president might want to do.

A participant in the task force process said: "If we just went in and presented something to him and left him to his own devices, I think we would end up with a version of let's go drop a bomb on the people who were trying to cross the border."

"During this period, Deb Birx [Dr. Deborah Birx, White House coronavirus coordinator] practically lived in the White House," Fauci said. "She had an office in the lower level of the West Wing. She was killing herself and there was a lot of pressure on her. That was her full-time job. So, when we realized in early March that we needed to take concrete steps to contain the spread of the virus, she and I decided that what we needed to do was to put together a program to essentially shut the country down for fifteen days. Our thinking was that [Trump] would not do more than that. But we felt, let's at least get him to say fifteen days.

"That was something we learned how to do with him. Do things little by little. Because, if we said we need to shut down for forty-five days, he'd just say, 'Get out of the office, don't even think about it.' But we said, 'Why don't we do it for fifteen days?' And we knew that at the end of fifteen days we never would have had enough data to be able to say, 'We are done, let's move on.' So, when we got to the end of the fifteen days, we put together another plan, a thirty-day extension. And that helped. That helped flatten the curve.

"Now, to the president's credit, when we presented the thirty-day extension of the fifteen days, the economics people really didn't like that. Mnuchin didn't like it. Kudlow didn't like it. But the president did it anyway. And I thought, 'We really got him on our side.' But then somebody must have spoken to him, I think, because a day and a half later he tweets, saying, 'Liberate Virginia! Liberate Michigan!' Which [many] governors took as a sign to abandon that thirty-day plan, and do whatever you want. Which was the beginning of the political divide on this that we still see today. That was the problem."

Olivia Troye, like others on the task force or with whom I spoke on background, confirmed this scenario. Troye said: "Birx at the very beginning pushes the fifteen days to slow the spread. I mean, she falls on her sword for that with Pence to make that happen. So, Pence and her go in and fight for it, and win by some miracle of God. But it didn't matter. Because right after it Trump doubles down and starts pressuring governors to open up the country. You see what I mean? So it doesn't matter. Any good work that was done towards the beginning of it didn't matter. Because what was happening that was countering it was so detrimental that we were never going to succeed. And it was not going to allow the country to unify against this virus."

In other words, as quickly as the team assigned to lead the fight against the virus could come up with ways to get the president to embrace sound policies, he would undo them. But the fifteen days to stop the spread strategy did ultimately have a net positive effect in reducing the speed of the disease's spread.

There were other ways Trump would personally disrupt the process. One task force participant recalled: "He would like, crash the party. So sometimes he would derail the whole thing we had planned with meetings or briefings. When he would show up, it would just change the entire thing. You lose control over the event. If Trump attended, after a while it became clear that the session was pointless." Consequently, as happened in other comparable circumstances, the participants would find ways to have discussions off line or privately. "It was not," said one, "insubordinate. It was just our instinct for survival kicking in. Just a way to actually get the work done, which in this case had big life-and-death stakes attached to it."

The fifteen-day program was not without its flaws. Some were tied to ignorance. It was as late as the end of February when the surgeon general Jerome Adams said: "Seriously people—stop buying masks! They are not effective in preventing the general public from catching coronavirus." His comments were not only wrong, but also related to another concern: the shortages of PPE for medical professionals. (He wanted to ensure there were enough masks for them.) At the time of the mid-March program launch, there had been only about four thousand reported cases of COVID in the United States. There was little understanding of how the disease was transmitted, or that it could be transmitted by people who were not showing symptoms.

Nor did the program incorporate sufficient recommendations for testing. In part, according to participants in the interagency process, due to Trump's antipathy for doing anything that might "make the numbers look bad." To avoid getting results he didn't want the president steered away from testing. That, of course, is precisely the opposite of what the scientific and medical outlook was and should have been. Further, the relative brevity of the original plan further undermined the state and local public health professionals' faith in White House efforts. While from the inside "fifteen days" looked like a good work-around and perhaps the best that could be gotten out of the president, on the outside it looked like the White House did not understand the gravity of the problem.

Saskia Popescu, an epidemiologist at George Mason University, was quoted by CNBC.com: "Truly for many of us in public health, this was a red flag—an indication that the administration had an unrealistic view of pandemic control measures and was not aware of the reality—a pandemic cannot be solved in fifteen days, and any strategy needs to include a serious amount of work resource and personnel."

The country was rocked by the virus during March 2020. The shutdown hit the economy hard. Trump and Mnuchin pushed through an "economic recovery" package, although once implemented it was a package that ultimately benefitted primarily corporations and the top 10 percent of the population. Popular figures like Tom Hanks caught the disease. Ten days after the launch of the plan, the US death toll hit one thousand, and the United States surpassed China in number of cases.

Meanwhile, through all of this Trump's and the administration's messages to the people were contradictory. When the plan started, Trump said: "With several weeks of focused action, we can turn the corner and turn it quickly." A couple of days later, he said: "To this day, nobody has seen anything like what they were able to do during World War II. And now it is our time. We must sacrifice together because we are all in this together, and we'll come through this together." Pundits began to ask (again) if he had finally become "presidential."

The disease spread even within the White House, which could not get its act together concerning protocols. Further travel bans to stop the spread were announced. But the president wanted the message to be positive. He had his FDA head announce that two drugs, remdesivir and hydroxychloroquine, were showing encouraging signs as treatments. But Trump also took flack for trying to shift blame by calling the disease the "China virus." (In doing so he was playing, on his own behalf, to racists and also to the China hawks in his administration.) And while the president had activated an act that allowed him to marshal private-sector resources in an emergency, he and the "leave it to the markets" purists on his team resisted using it: PPE shortages were followed by ventilator shortages.

Then Trump announced that his new goal was to open the country back up by Easter, a couple of weeks away at the time. The public health professionals in the administration were "aghast," "outraged," and "disgusted." Trump was pushing for political reasons. He had political rallies scheduled that he still wanted to be able to hold. But as Fauci said during a briefing at the time: "You don't make the timeline. The virus makes the timeline."

During a pandemic, messaging matters. In fact, careful communication is a central element of any coordinated policy response. Bad or inconsistent messaging can lead to panic or deep misunderstandings in the public sphere. Conflicting messages out of the White House led to renewed use of the word "infodemic," referring to the rapid dissemination of factual and nonfactual information about a topic. (I coined the term in a *Washington Post* op-ed about the SARS epidemic in 2003.)

In February of 2020, the World Health Organization had warned that part of the COVID problem was a "massive infodemic." In the same month, the *MIT Technology Review* called it "the first true social-media 'infodemic,'" saying new technologies had "zipped information and misinformation around the world at unprecedented speeds, fueling panic, racism . . . and hope."

Donald Trump was the Typhoid Mary of the COVID infodemic. Whatever obstacles he may have created for his team behind the scenes, whatever bad policies he may have promoted, he almost certainly did the most damage when he regularly took the podium during the spring of 2020. The problem for staff was the same with these live briefings as it was with his Twitter use: there was no way to stop him once he had disintermediated everyone who stood between him and his audience. Leon Panetta's admonition that Kelly throw away Trump's "tweeter" was not possible. And if that was the case, keeping Trump away from the cameras to which he was addicted was even harder. Because Trump was remarkably undisciplined, very suggestible, and surrounded by sycophants who played to his ego, it was very difficult for even dedicated, disciplined staff to keep him on message, though they tried.

One of the most notorious incidents took place in April of 2020 during one of Trump's nearly daily COVID press conferences. (Staff ultimately found the only way to keep Trump from repeating errors like the ones about to be described was to dissuade him from doing daily press conferences. Keeping him away from the podium was one of the best means of controlling a main driver of the COVID infodemic.)

Olivia Troye lays some of the blame for this incident at the feet of the vice president's communication director Katie Miller (Stephen Miller's wife). According to Troye: "Every day Katie Miller had to have a theme for the press conference. And we had briefed that study on some steps that might help reduce the spread of the virus around the house. And she goes in and fights for it to happen and says, 'We've got the study, we should talk about it. It's good news, yay, yay.' You know, that's Katie Miller. That's what she would do every day. And we were then like, 'Well, wait a second. You got to be careful what you're saying here. Like we're saying that maybe sunshine kills the virus on surfaces. Like, that's good news. So maybe being outdoors is better than being indoors. But we need to frame it properly."

The task force met for an hour to discuss how to present the new information, including Vice President Pence and Deborah Birx. So they were fully informed, as were the DHS scientists. Chad Wolf, acting secretary of Homeland Security, was also present. The group talked in depth about what the study was saying and what it wasn't saying—about household cleaners and bleach and how they worked on surfaces on the virus.

But then Troye observed, Katie Miller intervened: "Katie Miller decides that this is a good-news piece and runs down the hallway, pitches it, then they go in there and we decided this is going to be sunlight and bleach day for COVID. That's really how it happens. And I'm sitting right outside the Oval, and Trump is saying, 'Oh, well, this is a good thing. Let's get it out there.' The last thing in his ear before the press conference is 'bleach is good; sunlight's good.' And he gobbles it up in his darn head. And he goes out there and says, 'Inject bleach into your body, maybe you should do that,' like it'll kill the COVID. That is exactly what happens. And that is classic

Donald Trump. This White House can go from a very serious in-depth briefing of actual facts in policy and something that can be constructive, to completely getting derailed and going off the tracks. All within a matter of two hours."

Troye continued, describing what happened next: "I turned to Marc [Short]. I'm like, 'What did he just say?' And I'm watching the TV. And I see everyone looked at me and then I'm like, back to poker face. At that point, I just wanted to go home. I think I texted my husband and said, 'Are you watching this?' And all I could think was what's the point? I'm just gonna go home, but then I realized I can't go home because someone's going to kill themselves tonight, because they're going to follow [the president's] instructions. Because there are people out there who do everything that he tells him to do. So, somewhere there's gonna be a family that dies, someone's going to make a buck and start making bleach because that's what was happening during COVID. There were all these horrible things happening where people were making fake robes, fake masks. We were dealing with that, by the way, too. And I was dealing with all the contraband, all the big stuff on the market, the supply-chain issues. So, I realized I had to start dealing with that."

Deborah Birx had the misfortune to be sitting in the press room as Trump spoke the words about injecting bleach. She was on camera, and when Trump looked to her for validation she did not make any effort to correct or challenge him. As a consequence she appeared to validate him. It was a blow to her reputation from which she never fully recovered. Later, Dr. Fauci did in fact challenge Trump's ludicrous and dangerous assertion. Ultimately, it led to a kind of war against Fauci by the Trump insider team. They saw his having the integrity to stand up for the facts as disloyalty.

Fauci recalled: "When I started to really speak out to the press, when I would say I disagreed with what the president said, a very strange thing happened in the administration. The White House did a bizarre thing. They did opposition research on me. They looked at everything I said and tried to show that I was wrong a lot. So, we had the communications department of the White House sending out to all the networks, and all of the print media like the *New York Times* and the *Washington Post*, all things that they claimed show I don't know what I'm talking about. That is almost ludicrous—that you're working in a White House and the White House communication staff is sending out discrediting information to the press. So, I was not out there in the press conference that day, because I was being held back from interacting with the press. Poor Debbie Birx was out there with [the president]."

Fauci added: "When the guy from DHS who briefed us before that meeting, on [the recent findings about the effectiveness of bleach at eliminating the virus on surfaces], I thought it was a complete bunch of nonsense and would definitely be misinterpreted. And I made that clear in a civil, nonpejorative way, in the Situation Room; and Marc Short, who is a very reasonable person said, 'Well, if you feel a little concerned about it, then why don't we just not have you go out in the press room.' So I said, 'Fine by me, I'll go home.' And Deb went out. And that's when she inadvertently got sucked into that ridiculous show of drinking and injecting bleach into people. I was looking at the TV and I didn't realize that he was going to say that, but when he did I was saying to myself, 'Deb, get up and scream. Tell him he's full of shit.' But she didn't, and really could not under the circumstances. She was in a very tough spot."

Coping with Crazy

Elizabeth Neumann, an assistant secretary at DHS at the time, described how the "bleach" moment fit into her view of how the administration worked, more generally. She wondered what she was really seeing:

"'Is he doing the entertaining thing?' Because he will. He loves to just kind of riff and come up with bombastic things to get people to talk. So I couldn't tell in that moment. I'm listening to the bleach thing and wondering was that what he genuinely thinks? Because there were multiple moments when you'd be saying to yourself, 'I can't tell, is he actually that clueless?' Is putting alligators in moats really an option? Or can we use missiles against immigrant caravans? What would you say if you're in the room? And everybody's first instinct is to think, 'Look, you are the president of the United States. I'm going to treat you like the president of the United States.' How does one respond to that with appropriate respect for the office, when inside your brain you're going, 'I cannot believe this is happening.' And that happened more than you can imagine.

"At DHS, Kelly and Kristjen [Nielsen] would be coming back from meetings in the Oval Office, and they were very circumspect about what they would say. But their eyes would be wide. And then when DHS staff were preparing briefing materials for Kelly or Nielsen to present to the president, they'd say to us, 'We need to keep it really tight.' One slide, nothing more. Or he would become distracted. They wanted to avoid lengthy discussions. So we would need to have everything precoordinated. Anytime there was a decision meeting with the president, there was a lot of time spent with Mattis's staff, or with Tillerson's staff, to get everybody on the same page. And maybe, if there was a side benefit, it's probably because it led to DHS, State, and DOD agreeing on as many things as they did, because we all realized that if you put this in front of the president, disastrous decisions could occur. So we had to agree in advance on everything and hope, hope that he would take your recommendation, because if you open it up to too much discussion, you end up with these crazy and dangerous ideas."

Neumann continued: "Of course, that was not the only challenge. You'd have meetings with all the cabinet secretaries in alignment, with McMaster and the NSC in agreement, and you'd walk out, and everybody thinks they've got their marching orders. And then two hours later, Jared [Kushner] would come into the Oval Office with his big grand idea. And then just overturn whatever decision was just made with the NSC. Or if it wasn't Jared, it was Stephen [Miller]. There was no control on who could see the president. It could be Lou Dobbs that night, or it could be Sean Hannity—whatever they said that night would become the president's policy the next morning. These unpredictable outside influencers that were allowed to dictate policy, even after decisions had been made. And we saw that effect constantly. I can't remember if it was Kelly or Nielsen, but one of them was in Mexico trying to negotiate something, and Trump tweeted something and just kind of pulled the rug, totally botched the trip. We couldn't get anything done."

For Neumann and her peers it was immensely frustrating that Trump seemed to want to be an entertainer as much as a president, and that he showed "complete disrespect for the fact that anything that government did actually had value." To get serious work done and keep the president if not on board then at least out of the way, bizarre shifting coalitions developed to offset the destabilizing influence of Jared Kushner and

Stephen Miller: "Sometimes you could triangulate, usually in partnership with the chief of staff and maybe the national security advisor, or then maybe you could get Ivanka or Jared or somebody else. I mean, believe it or not, senior staff from the agencies often went to Melania for help."

"Here we were trying to address one of the biggest challenges the nation could possibly face," said one participant in the Task Force process. "And at the same time our work was being perpetually undermined from within because, for example, the president was in bed with Fox [News] or Fox was in bed with the president. You had Fox contradicting most of the things we were trying to do from a public health standpoint. When you're trying to do something that most of the time is diametrically opposite to what Fox is talking about, it was like, 'How are we going to win this war?'"

One of the other "distractions" that also colored the conversation was Trump's desire to bring corporations into the mix, to create the image of a more private sector–driven response to the pandemic. As part of this, Trump would host meetings with CEOs, and even press events where the CEOs would play a kind of show-and-tell game displaying products or listing steps they were taking to help fight the disease, while also heaping fulsome praise on Trump.

Fauci adds: "At some point, of course, [White House chief of staff] Mark Meadows became very angry with me and he would block my going on the networks and on cable. And what I would do is I would give a podcast to Harvard University, and CNN would then pick it up and run the entire podcast. So even though he said you can't go on CNN, I would be on CNN for twenty minutes anyway. That's when things really got very, very tense between me and the White House towards the end."

Like other senior staffers, Fauci also found other ways to get critical work done fighting the pandemic, even when the inner circle in the White House was hostile or dysfunctional. For example, he says: "I had a very good relationship with the governors, particularly the Democratic governors. I mean, Phil Murphy from New Jersey would call me up all the time for advice, as would John Bell Edwards from Louisiana, Andrew Cuomo from New York, among others. However, the regular calls with the group of governors run by the vice president and sometimes the president were often tough to take. They would often start off with a Republican governor saying, 'Mr. President, you are doing an amazing job. I mean, we just love what you're doing. Congratulations, blah, blah, blah.' And then that would be it. Instead of saying, 'By the way, I'm having twenty thousand cases a day in my state, what are we going to do about it?' it was 'What a great job you're doing.' So the work-around with the governors was that I would just get on the phone separately from the vice president's or president's call with the governors and talk to them. They would call me up and say, 'Tony, give me some advice. What should we be doing?' and I tried to be of help in that way."

Olivia Troye witnessed the growing disconnect of the president's inner circle as his reelection campaign kicked into gear. After July [2021]: "Pence starts to change his demeanor, too. Because I see him go from really taking this seriously—he's in the meetings, he's running them, he's trying to take action on things. But in the summer that changed. It was like watching Pence transform into a totally different person right before my eyes. And his chief of staff, Marc Short, could not wait to get on the road. He was so sick of this. It was hard to even get him to pick up the phone. Sometimes, from that point on, I would make decisions on my own because I had no choice."

Politics, of course, had always been the name of the game in dealing with the pandemic, as far as Trump was concerned. One member of the cabinet said to me: "I think he came to hate the pandemic more for what he saw it was doing to his election chances than what it was doing to the country. I know that's harsh. But he was very focused on himself." It had colored the way Trump waged his war against data, resisting testing, strong-arming the CDC to downplay threats and numbers. It colored the way his inner circle handled needs from different states, as illustrated by Jared Kushner's famous comment in a meeting when, according to *Vanity Fair*, he lashed out against New York governor Andrew Cuomo, a Democrat, saying: "Cuomo didn't pound the phones hard enough to get PPE for his state. His people are going to suffer, and that's their problem."

Kushner's desire to delegate the response to the states or the private sector was also an effort to get the stain of the pandemic off of his father-in-law. "The federal government is not going to lead this response. It's up to the states to figure out what they want to do," was just one of many statements from him in this vein. Another, also recounted by *Vanity Fair*, was "Free markets will solve this. That is not the role of government." Kushner also argued behind the scenes that because at the outset COVID was hitting blue states hardest, a national plan was not needed; the absence of a national plan in fact would be beneficial—any blame would fall on blue-state governors.

Politics helped the inner circle decide who would get special help from the government. One senior White House staffer said: "Meadows didn't want to deal with it. The only time he did was when a big constituent called and was complaining. Like if one of the Republican senators called him and was pissed off about what was happening to cruise ships. His office would call me and say, 'Someone's upset about cruise ships and crew members. Do something about it.' In the end, I think Trump and the team closest to him, his political advisors, were really just angry it was impacting their ability to navigate the [2020 reelection] campaign."

Ultimately, perhaps the pandemic itself ended up putting an end to Trump's anti-science impulses and crazy suggestions in a way that none among even the most resourceful members of his administration could. Because if there was one single factor that led to Trump's defeat, it was probably his mishandling of COVID.

One of Trump's own pollsters, Tony Fabrizio, issued a postmortem analysis of why Trump lost his reelection bid. In ten key states, voters ranked the COVID pandemic as the crucial election issue. And Joe Biden won the support of voters who shared that concern by a three to one margin. The same analysis revealed that a majority of voters disapproved of Trump's response to the pandemic. So in the end democracy was the ultimate guardrail.

But Trump and his inner circle had a plan for that, too.

CHAPTER SIX

The Deep State Versus
the Dark State

Liberty lies in the hearts of men and women;

when it dies there, no constitution, no law, no court

can save it . . . while it lies there, it needs no

constitution, no law, no court to save it.

—LEARNED HAND, JURIST

B Y MAY 25, 2020, more than 98,000 people in the
United States had died of COVID. More than 1.6
million cases of the disease had been reported. It was,
however, Memorial Day and Americans, frustrated by lockdowns, crowded onto beaches and into parks despite the risks.

Thanks to the brutal economic downturn and skyrocket-
ing unemployment rates, frustrations nationwide were running high. The president, worried about how the economic
and health crises would impact his reelection chances, was
desperate to change the subject. For the first time in nearly
three months he played golf that weekend, at his company's

golf course in Sterling, Virginia. He and his golfing partners did not wear masks.

Over the weekend, Trump was active on social media. He tweeted or retweeted more than a hundred messages. It was the usual smorgasbord of Trump outbursts: attacking opponents, denouncing the "Russia hoax," promoting quack cures for COVID, and then, per custom, on Memorial Day he made a show of respect for the military with a visit to Arlington National Cemetery. Soon he would find a new and deeply disturbing way to disrespect the military, earning the opprobrium even of senior active and retired officers, men trained all their lives to stay out of politics and not publicly criticize their commander in chief.

The first trigger came from far outside the Washington Beltway, in Minneapolis, Minnesota, at eight o'clock on the evening of May 25. A forty-six-year-old black man named George Floyd was stopped by police on suspicion of having paid for some cigarettes with a counterfeit $20 bill. Floyd was removed from his vehicle at gunpoint and placed under arrest. When police attempted to put him in their patrol car, he pleaded with them not to do so, asserting he was anxious and claustrophobic. He was put in the car against his will, then a struggle ensued after which he was forced to the ground outside the car. Police officer Derek Chauvin then sought to subdue Floyd by placing his knee on Floyd's neck. Floyd protested, complaining that he could not breathe, and after a few moments stopped moving. Onlookers were recording the incident. An ambulance was called. Efforts to resuscitate Floyd failed. He was pronounced dead at 9:25 p.m.

Within hours, videos of Floyd's brutal murder at the hands of police went viral. The nation, already tense due to the twin economic and public health crises, was soon confronted with social unrest from coast to coast. Protests that began on May 26 in Minneapolis-St. Paul spread rapidly. Within days, over two hundred cities had imposed curfews. Within just a couple of weeks, over two thousand US cities, and dozens worldwide, had witnessed Black Lives Matter (BLM) protests.

Trump saw this as an opportunity to dust off several tried-and-true racist themes from his 2016 campaign and the first part of his presidency. He regularly had derided the Black Lives Matter movement, those who supported it, and the unrest that came from protests condemning America's institutional racism, in particular police departments' record of brutality. At rallies, Trump would even support the idea of violence against Black Lives Matter protestors. In response to the protests, on May 28 he tweeted: "These THUGS are dishonoring the memory of George Floyd, and I won't let that happen."

The next evening protestors convened in Lafayette Park, directly across the street from the White House. Trump was in residence. The Secret Service and police skirmished with the crowd. Eleven Secret Service agents were transported to the hospital. At that point, with the White House complex in lockdown, the Secret Service suggested Trump and his family relocate to the secure bunker located under the executive mansion. The next morning he tweeted that had protestors breached the White House grounds, they would have been "greeted with the most vicious dogs, the most ominous weapons I have ever seen." But the effort to appear tough and in control didn't work. The ensuing coverage of Trump's roughly hour-long stay in the bunker, which the president felt made him look weak, because it did, was unfavorable. He was angry as a result, really angry. According to *Washington Post* reporters Carol Leonnig and Philip Rucker in their book *I*

Alone Can Fix It, Trump demanded to know who had leaked the story and ranted that they should be tried for treason. He searched for ideas to change the narrative.

Trump met with his team, including Secretary of Defense Mark Esper, Chairman of the Joint Chiefs of Staff Mark Milley, White House Chief of Staff Mark Meadows, Stephen Miller, and others in the Oval Office to discuss how to respond to the protests. Leonnig and Rucker report Stephen Miller said: "Mr. President, you have to show strength. They're burning the country down." Milley responded: "Stephen, shut the fuck up. They're not burning the fucking country down." Trump nonetheless pushed for military intervention. Milley argued it was not needed. In a subsequent meeting, Miller asserted the demonstrations were an insurrection warranting the use of troops. (His assertion was based on the Insurrection Act of 1807, which allows for the deployment of US military forces within the country under very narrow circumstances, such as quelling civil unrest.) Again, Milley pushed back. He and Esper were deeply unsettled by Trump's appetite to deploy troops to suppress citizens who were simply exercising their First Amendment rights.

On the morning of June 1, the president again reconvened his advisors, this time also including Attorney General Bill Barr. Trump argued that the riots were making the United States look weak to foreign countries. He again raised the issue of deploying troops, maybe even the 82nd Airborne Division, to quiet the unrest in Washington. Defense Secretary Esper argued that this was a job for the police, for local law enforcement. Trump was furious at the pushback he was getting. Milley raised the issue of the constitutional right to protest. Trump fulminated. Vice President Pence, as was his wont, sat like a mannequin. Barr, whom the president had seen as one of his go-to problem solvers, sided with the military and DOD leadership. Esper, eager to do anything to keep active-duty forces off the streets, offered to see if he could encourage governors to mobilize the National Guard. Barr offered some "reinforcements" from the law enforcement agencies he controlled. At a moment of crisis, over and over again through the Trump years, this was what managing Trump looked like: absorbing his blows, laying out the facts, side-stepping his most extreme and often illegal suggestions, and searching for ways to give him the semblance of a win, since that seemed to be the only way to placate him.

After the meetings and a subsequent teleconference with governors, during which Trump simply ignored his team's advice, his team met privately to try to figure out how to deal with both the situation in the streets and the commander in chief, who seemed dedicated to the idea of escalating the protests into a full-fledged constitutional crisis.

Later on June 1, Ivanka Trump presented her father with a plan to help strengthen his image. A small fire had occurred across the street from the White House in St. John's Church, just on the other side of Lafayette Park. It had allegedly been started by the protestors. According to a White House staffer there at the time, his impression was that Ivanka was trying to manage her father, to get him to set aside his most confrontational impulses and to do something that would appear more benign and healing. She encouraged him to go to the church and pray as a way to demonstrate he was seeking to unite the nation. Ultimately, Trump agreed to walk the short distance to the church for a photo op. He would carry a Bible with him, brandishing it for the cameras.

It was not, however, the symbolism of Trump holding up a Bible in front of a church, laughably cynical as it was given his lack of religious convictions, that ended up being a source of controversy. It was that by having Esper and Milley accompany him on his walk across the park, Trump once again sent a message that the military was part of his plan to stabilize the nation and quell the protests. That, combined with the show of force involved in clearing the park to make the photo op possible, ignited a firestorm over the authoritarian impulses of America's forty-fifth president. By extension, those impulses were ascribed to the advisors who had accompanied him on the short walk from the White House to St. Johns, a group that also included Barr. It also triggered serious criticism of Esper's and Milley's judgment, despite whatever they may have said behind the scenes, for accompanying Trump on his PR stroll. They both later admitted they were deeply uncomfortable with the way they were being used by the commander in chief. In fact, Milley told Esper he wasn't going to be part of the spectacle; he simply stopped walking with the president and headed off to speak with some of the national guardsmen nearby.

According to *Peril* by Bob Woodward and Robert Costa, on the walk over, Esper turned to Milley and said: "We've been duped. We're being used." And Milley said to his chief of staff: "This is fucked up and this is a political event and I'm out of here. We're getting the fuck out of here. I'm fucking done with this shit."

The flack Esper and Milley got was intense, and much of it came from sources close to the military. Former defense secretary James Mattis, who since resigning had taken criticism for remaining largely silent on his concerns about Trump, wrote in a letter published by the *Atlantic* that he was "angry and appalled" by the scenes in Lafayette Park. He made it very clear that in his view the military should be used at home only on "very rare occasions." Mattis was especially angry because the US military, a uniquely apolitical institution, was being commandeered by a president with uniquely divisive instincts: "Donald Trump is the first president in my lifetime who does not try to unite the American people—does not even pretend to try. Instead, he tries to divide us."

A week later, in a prerecorded address to students at the National Defense University, Milley apologized. Stating that he had lost his sense of "situational awareness" that evening in Lafayette Park, he went on to say: "Many of you saw the results of the photograph of me in Lafayette Square last week, that sparked a national debate about the role of the military in civil society. I should not have been there. My presence in that moment, and in that environment, created the perception of the military involved in domestic politics."

Months afterward, Kori Schake, one of the country's leading experts on civilian-military relations, cited the Lafayette Park event as another example of Trump exploiting the military. She said: "I think Mark was genuinely shocked at the president trying to get them to go kill peaceful protesters, and wanting hordes of airborne rangers parachuting in to clear crowds. Why that triggered Mark is because he saw what that would do to the American public's relationship with its military. And that more than anything was where he pivots. He starts being intensely worried about what it will do to the relationship between the American public and its military to have its military be seen as a political arm of the presidency."

In the wake of the event, Esper and Milley struggled with balancing their sense of duty with their deep concern with the way Trump was handling the situation. Milley considered resigning. Esper and Milley knew each other well, having served side by side for two years when Esper was secretary of the army and Milley was chief of staff for the army. Esper said: "General Milley and I had a close relationship, having already worked together for nearly two years before taking on our respective roles atop the Pentagon. This was probably unique in the history of secretaries of defense and chairmen of the joint chiefs. Having that trust, confidence, and understanding of one another was important, especially in the Trump administration, and during the toughest days of our time together. I could close the door and say anything I wanted to him, and vice versa, despite the fact that we often knew exactly what the other was thinking. When it came to the proper role of DOD in elections, dealing with civil unrest, and so on, we were completely aligned. We both agreed on the importance of keeping the military apolitical and getting the department through November 2nd without incident. I didn't want the troops in the streets of Portland, Seattle, or anywhere else for that matter, whether before, during, or after the election. Dealing with civil unrest was the proper domain of civilian law enforcement, not DOD."

War Games

Milley and Esper were not alone in their concerns. In fact, in the prior autumn a group of former national security officials and others with experience at the highest levels in Washington had come together to form the Transition Integrity Project. Their goal was to explore scenarios that might occur if Trump and his supporters contested an election result.

During June of 2020, days after the Lafayette Park debacle, almost seventy of them linked up to conduct a series of "war games." Rosa Brooks was a former Defense Department official. Like Schake, she had also been a regular panelist for the *Deep State Radio* podcasts since the show's inception in mid-2017. In an interview with *USA Today* she said: "The goal was to illuminate what could happen. We don't have the ability to say, 'Is there a one percent chance that these bad outcomes occur, or an 80 percent?' But the collective wisdom is that they are sufficiently high probability that we can't afford not to be thinking about them at least."

With Nils Gilman, a scholar at the Berggruen Institute, and Brooks (who is also a constitutional scholar and who holds the Scott K. Ginsburg chair in law and policy at Georgetown University Law Center), the group organized four different scenarios that explored a range of possible outcomes: a clear-cut win for Biden; a narrow win for Biden; a close win for Trump but that came with a slim popular vote loss; and a contested vote from which the winner was hard to determine for weeks. With the participants joining into groups representing the different campaigns, law enforcement, the military, and party officials, they considered how individuals and organizations might react. Some of the participants later said they were shocked at how naked power might be employed and that so many thought it likely.

The objective of the exercise was not to accurately predict what might happen, but rather was intended to help prepare people's thinking. However, the reality was that many elements of the scenarios proved uncannily accurate. Their core conclusion was that there was a great deal Trump could do to muddy the waters around the election, and even challenge its outcome. Further, there were few effective responses to what Trump might do, because courts were lethargic, political leaders were often timid, and Trump could populate the government with senior officials who would do his bidding or look the other way if he was bending the law.

While all of the scenarios were based on the election itself, the real challenge came if Trump tried to contest the results— if he were to argue that they were illegitimate and sought to overturn them by manipulating the processes in the Electoral College or Congress. Apparently, while the scenarios did not show Trump able to reverse the results in the weeks immediately after the election, they revealed a "pressure point" on which plans to undermine the election might well focus. A *USA Today* summary of their work framed that moment in the process in one of its subheads: "The Date to Watch: Jan. 6." That was when Biden would be officially named the winner by Congress. But if Trump, aided by his vice president, could stall the process or accept alternative electoral slates, deeper problems would ensue.

During the Trump years, Rosa Brooks was often asked on our podcast whether the United States was in the midst of a constitutional crisis yet, and she would typically say: "Not yet." But after she concluded the election exercises, she was deeply concerned that one might truly be on the horizon. With good reason.

Some folks were not so sure. In the same August *USA Today* article that pinpointed January 6 as the date to watch, former George W. Bush spokesperson Ari Fleischer dismissed the most extreme scenarios, saying: "I'm perfectly willing, and I do so often, to criticize Donald Trump. But this is pernicious. This is beyond the call. You talk about being divisive." He then suggested the idea that Trump might not accept the election results was "dangerous." He was right, of course. Just not in the way he meant to be. (As of this writing in the spring of 2022, Donald Trump has yet to accept the election results.)

What is striking is that Washington insiders' concerns were being echoed within the administration among people like Esper and Milley. And they were not alone. Indeed, concerns about how Trump would handle the next election had swirled among his top officials, once it was clear the Russians had interfered with the 2016 results. So just as Esper, Milley, Barr, and the others had met to figure out how to contain the president's impulse to drop paratroopers into the streets to silence BLM protestors, other groups had worked together at a high level to remove a potential trigger for the unrest the Transition Integrity Project was most concerned about: cyber meddling in the election that might alter results, or at least lead to the kinds of disputes regarding outcomes that Trump could exploit.

Those efforts proved more successful than attempts to keep Trump from trying to flex military muscle in the wake of the George Floyd protests. The roots had been planted in the earliest days of the Trump administration, when in the wake of the infamous meeting in the Pentagon's Tank, senior officials were shaken. One senior Trump administration official told me: "The reaction was 'Oh my God, this is scary. We're in a scary place when that kind of meeting happens.'"

As a consequence, on an irregular but ongoing basis top officials would consult with one another casually, or in meetings that were neither part of the official policy process nor known to the White House. In these meetings cabinet secretaries and sometimes their most senior advisors could be candid, confident their views would remain within the group. Such conversations take place in all administrations; it is the natural process of colleagues communicating and getting to know each other. Sometimes the meetings are more formally acknowledged and process adjacent, like the un-Group that met within the NSC of the George H. W. Bush administration, the Albright-Berger-Cohen meetings of the Clinton years, or similar regular check-in sessions with senior officials. Sometimes they are far more casual and based on friendships or old school ties. One Trump cabinet member downplayed the discussions, saying: "It's not like we had a club and we had a secret password to get into the club. There were just a few of us that would call each other and try as best we could to work problems out together."

Kirstjen Nielsen explained how working with such a group would fit into her way of handling challenges from the White House: "I had two or three strategies for trying to work with the president. One was to always try to give him alternatives. Because if I could understand what he was really trying to get done or the message he was trying to send, I would try and help to find a way to do what he was wanting to do in a way that made sense from the perspective of what legal authorities we might actually have and that were in line with resources and operational realties. I also tried in every instance to give him a broader view of the consequences of suggested actions on different stakeholders, international relations, trade and the economy, etc. There are often multiple ways to achieve an objective and rocking all the boats to achieve it is rarely the best policy, in my mind.

"Another way was to have a call list in my head for when things started to go off the rails. For example, there were times when he would be upset with Puerto Rico or California and he didn't want to give them aid after a federal disaster was declared—a hurricane in one case, forest fires in the other. So, first of all, it's not discretionary. Once the President declares a disaster, the aid and support automatically kicks in, consistent with the Stafford Act. It's not discretionary and, therefore, it's certainly not a political decision. So in those cases, I would use that call list. And I would call, for example, Kevin McCarthy and say, 'Kevin, you've got to call the president.'"

Nielsen continued reflectively: "I did my best, but I'm one voice. And (the President) generally, it's pretty well known, was very frustrated that DHS did more than border security and was very frustrated that I could not 'secure the border' by simply 'refusing to let people in.' Yelling was not out of the ordinary. So, when I couldn't persuade him on my own, I'd have a list to call, depending on what the topic was. And they would call and back me up or, sometimes, I'd ask that they not even mention they had spoken to me at all if I felt that the positive effect would be greater the second way." She noted that while there were certainly people she could count on, there were others she did not consider particularly helpful. Either they did not want to cross the president or they were actually part of the loyalist group closest to him.

A senior Trump administration official outlined a process I heard described by others in Trump's cabinet and sub-cabinet: "There were informal conversations amongst the cabinet. Refugees was a good example. We went back and forth a lot trying to end up in a better place via back-channel conversations." The official notes that in that particular case, the process was not successful at redirecting the policy discussion.

One area in which the informal process was especially important was election security. It was a very difficult issue to discuss with the president. One senior law enforcement official said to me: "It was a no-fly-zone with Trump. He would shoot you down the minute you brought it up. It was because of Russia and 2016. Anytime you brought it up he reflexively thought you were questioning his legitimacy."

A Trump NSC official observed to me that John Bolton, when he was national security advisor, would not hold meetings about election security. "He had a radar about what could and could not be productively discussed with the president, and he was careful not to lose points with the Oval by getting bogged down in topics that unleashed the president's neuroses."

Nielsen echoed this awareness and then described a shadow process that evolved as a consequence: "The White House didn't want to talk about it. There was this belief, which I think is probably true, that if you started to talk about elections at all, it would trigger the president to go into his standard defensive comments that he won the election in 2016 and so on. In fact, DNI Coats and I had to negotiate with the WH so that he, FBI Director Wray, and I could brief Congress on the threat. I also drafted a memo to other Cabinet Members on the subject—because we had an important election security mandate at DHS and the lanes between DOJ, State, the Intel community and DHS were not clear at the time. And per the memo, I started organizing and hosting a separate NSC-like process. I let the White House know. It's not that I did it in secret. But candidly, they did not want to get involved. The highest-ranking person they would send at one point was Mira Ricardel, who was not deeply engaged in the substance but did collaborate on the communications." (Ricardel served at the time as deputy national security advisor. She was given the cybersecurity brief, but within the cybersecurity community the appointment was controversial because she was not seen as especially knowledgeable on the subject. Also, although she was brought into the White House by Bolton, she had a combative relationship with other agencies and ultimately, in a strange twist, was pushed out of her job by the First Lady, Melania Trump, for allegedly being responsible for leaks about her.)

Other original members of the group included Director of National Intelligence Dan Coats, National Security Agency

Director and Commander of US Cyber Command General Paul Nakasone, Defense Secretary Mattis, FBI Director Christopher Wray, and at the outset, Deputy Attorney General Rod Rosenstein (although reportedly he withdrew early from these conversations). Nielsen described the process as independent and producing its own sets of "deliverables" based on the participants' agreement. ("Deliverables" is Washington-speak for concrete outcomes: the alternative to meetings or government efforts that merely produce talk or more process.) The participants did feel as though they had a statutory responsibility to report their work to Congress. When Nielsen informed Congress that she, Wray, and a representative from the Office of the Director of National Intelligence would go and brief them, a source familiar with the White House reaction said the president's inner circle "had a heart attack." But the group proceeded anyway because they felt it was the right thing to do, as well as their legal obligation.

Other participants included Chris Krebs, who played a central role on cybersecurity issues at DHS and in the administration. Many with whom I spoke credit him for doing vital heavy lifting to ensure the 2020 elections were as secure as they turned out to be. Coming from the private sector, Krebs had joined the DHS in 2017 as senior counselor to the secretary of DHS. Subsequently he served as assistant secretary for infrastructure protection and later as the first director of the DHS's Cybersecurity and Infrastructure Security Agency (CISA). One White House official who admired Krebs's work called him a "behind-the-scenes hero" for playing such a central role in ensuring election security.

From the outset, the group had three core objectives: (1) to ensure responsibilities were clear with regard to preventing the hacking of critical election infrastructure; this was despite the fact that officials in the White House reportedly pushed back on categorizing the mechanisms of elections as "critical infrastructure"; (2) to combat foreign influence in the elections, with the FBI in the lead and with a crucial role to be played by the Intelligence Community; (3) coordinating efforts and making sure people knew what other agencies were doing, especially including, when necessary, the public. This third objective would traditionally have been handled through a White House–led process, but could not be because of high-level obstruction.

Nielsen explained why coordination and the role the group played, even in the early days, was so important: "Maybe a month after I became secretary, just as an example, I had given a speech to a group of diplomats on what our priorities were at Homeland Security. It was very heavy on cyber. And it was very heavy on the role Vladimir Putin had played interfering in the 2016 elections. I was making the point that we were stepping up our efforts, moving from complacency to ensuring there would be consequences for those behind election hacks and disinformation efforts. The Russian ambassador got up in the middle of the speech and walked out. And then I had three days of phone calls from the White House saying I was 'off message' and that no one had given me permission to say what I had, that I had not used the correct talking points. And all this was after the DNI report on election interference had already been issued. I was saying what the entire intelligence and law enforcement community had agreed was accurate."

That was not an atypical reaction for the White House on this set of issues. Similarly, when in 2018 as the midterm elections were approaching, a *Washington Post* story drew attention to the work being done, Bolton felt, in the words of one participant, "embarrassed that he did not play a bigger role."

And so he reached out and tried to wrest some control back to the White House. So it was agreed that Bolton, Nielsen, Wray, Nakasone (General Paul Nakasone, head of the National Security Agency and US Cybercommand), and Coats would give a White House briefing on the work being done. Their message was in part to the Russians. It was a warning to not meddle, and to underscore how prepared the United States was to rebuff efforts at interference.

In the words of a senior official involved in helping to prepare the event: "It was obviously the right thing to do. In any other administration it would have been a total no-brainer, a nonevent. But boy, was Trump pissed. It was like, 'Why the fuck did you guys have a press conference on this? Why the fuck are we wasting our time talking about this?' I mean, he was so mad. But he didn't know enough to know what to do to keep us from protecting the elections. And so it was just another thing he was pissed about, because it had some connection to Russia.

"But things continued on the work, and I give Coats a lot of credit on this, like on everything else. That guy was a real patriot. Because he took a lot of withering fire in these private meetings with Trump about the conclusions they reach on Russia and on the nature of ongoing Russian threats. And he would just take the hits over and over again. We were all so surprised Dan Coats lasted until he did, because I can remember in spring of 2018 thinking, 'His head's on the chopping block, he's gone.' And then he just kept hanging in there and doing his job, telling the truth, not being intimidated.

"And, believe it or not, on a number of occasions it was Mike Pence that was stepping in to help him out. The shared Indiana connection made a difference. Now, I want to be absolutely clear about this. Pence was a coward in almost every other respect. But the one place where he kind of stuck his neck out was if the issue or the person involved was very Hoosier. He feels strong about people from Indiana. That's probably a result of him having run for governor two times."

After Nielsen and some of the other original participants left the government, the framework stayed in place. More of the sessions were reportedly led at Krebs's level, among top members of the sub-cabinet. The process stayed informal, even while in other administrations it might have taken on a more formal standing within the broader NSC process. And within that process much work got done to ensure the 2020 elections were secure, an effort that of course intensified as the election approached.

During the course of 2020 this effort, spearheaded by the CISA but working in close conjunction with the Intelligence Community and other agencies, included continuing close coordination with state and local officials and briefing Congress. According to Krebs's testimony to Congress following the election, CISA "became aware of election-related adversary activity, including by Russia." This included Russia penetrating "election-related systems" in the United States and extracting information. Information was shared with authorities and the plots were foiled. As Krebs would also testify: "In no case did the Russians access any voting machines, tabulators, or equipment related to vote casting, counting, or certification."

The efforts also included steps to counter disinformation. One element was the Rumor Control website, which flagged public efforts to spread misinformation and counteract false claims. Krebs's testimony in mid-December 2020 to the Senate Committee on Homeland Security and Governmental Affairs also noted the following:

"The Rumor Control website had an early test. Just as we got it up and running, email messages allegedly from the Proud Boys—the far-right political organization—started showing up in voters' inboxes across the country. The emails appeared to target Democratic voters, threatening potential consequences if they did not cast votes in the election for President Trump. Of course, ballot secrecy is the law in all fifty states, meaning that there would be no feasible way to carry out the threats in these emails. To educate voters about ballot secrecy and ensure they understood that they could safely cast votes for the candidate of their choice, we worked quickly to post a Rumor Control entry about the subject on the website.

"The very next day, another round of malicious emails were sent to voters. This time, the emails included a link to an alleged Proud Boys video that purported to show someone hacking a voter registration database and accessing federal write-in absentee ballots (FWAB), which are typically used by military and overseas voters who requested but did not yet receive their absentee ballots. We got to work on two Rumor Control entries, one on email spoofing, to help voters understand that the Proud Boys did not actually send the emails in question, and another on FWAB, to help voters understand the security measures in place that relate to such ballots."

He added that "as we moved on from Election Day, we began to see wild and baseless domestic claims of hackers and malicious algorithms that flipped the vote in states across the country, singling out election equipment vendors for allegedly having ties to deceased foreign dictators. None of these claims matched up with what we knew about the facts."

Unfortunately for the United States and for a public well served by Krebs, CISA, and other members of the long-standing low-key effort to ensure election security—despite the ongoing

lack of cooperation and open hostility of the White House—
by the time Krebs gave his testimony, neither he nor many of
the people initially responsible for the effort were still working
in the government. As most Americans would subsequently
learn, the false claims Krebs cited being made to subvert public faith in the election results were actually part of an effort
led by the president of the United States himself that has become widely known as the Big Lie.

Krebs lost his job shortly after the election for doing the
one thing the Big Lie could not tolerate: telling the truth. He
described in a *Washington Post* column what happened after
Trump dismissed him via tweet: "On Monday, a lawyer for
the president's campaign [Joe diGenova] plainly stated that I
should be executed. I am not going to be intimidated by these
threats from telling the truth to the American people."

(Note: diGenova during an interview on *The Howie Carr
Show* said that Krebs was "a class-A moron. He should be
drawn and quartered. Taken out at dawn and shot.")

Krebs's firing was part of an increasingly bold effort by
Trump to purge the government of officials who did exactly
what Krebs had done. They spoke the truth. They did their
jobs. Many of them were Trump appointees. But they did not
place their loyalty to one individual above their professional
duties and responsibilities. As former DHS secretary Michael
Chertoff told me: "CISA in particular were up-front about the
threats that might interfere with the election, and then later
about the fact that there had not been any disruption of the
election process. I think they demonstrated themselves to be
faithful to their principles."

In many cases, these individuals were replaced by people
whose primary qualification for the job was perceived loyalty
to Trump. Again, what was happening was precisely what

many in the administration had feared—and what the Transition Integrity Project had predicted.

The constant attrition directed at decent professionals claimed Dan Coats in late 2019. His regular challenges to the president had become too much. Earlier in 2019, he had testified to a Senate panel that Iran was not yet seeking a nuclear weapon; that ISIS remained active in Syria and Iraq; and that North Korea was not likely to give up its nuclear weapons. It was as if he had gone through a checklist of Trump claims and debunked each of them sequentially. He resigned effective August 15 of that year. Trump nominated as his replacement Republican Rep. John Ratcliffe, a Texas congressman known primarily as a defender of Trump's. Contrary to the statutory requirements for the job, Ratcliffe did not have extensive intelligence experience. Even Senate Republicans were uneasy with the nomination, especially after it was revealed that Ratcliffe, a former prosecutor, had lied about his counterterrorism experience in that job.

In early August, Trump withdrew the Ratcliffe nomination. The job should have by statute gone to Coats's very highly respected deputy, Sue Gordon, but Trump did not wish to have her serve in that capacity. So she too resigned when Coats left. Trump then chose a path he was increasingly coming to favor. By selecting candidates to serve in an "acting" rather than permanent role, he obviated the need to go through contentious confirmation hearings. This allowed him to put in place people he was more comfortable with. His first choice to serve as acting DNI was Joseph Maguire, a retired vice admiral who had led the National Counterterrorism Center.

Unfortunately for Trump, Maguire also took the job seriously and insisted the team around him do so as well. On

February 13, 2020, one of Maguire's staffers, Shelby Pierson, testified to the House Intelligence Committee that Russia was already interfering in the 2020 election, and was doing so with a "preference" for Trump. According to a person who saw his reaction, the president "got red in the face and exploded." He took it out on Maguire and then immediately announced Maguire would be replaced by Richard Grenell, who was serving as US ambassador in Germany.

Grenell was a poster boy for the new look Trump wanted. He was loyal to Trump to a fault, unscrupulous, willing to lie for the president, eager to purge others who did not share Trump's views, and—the ultimate recommendation for a manifestly ignorant president—completely unqualified for the job, with zero experience in the Intelligence Community. Grenell would keep his diplomatic post—where he regularly infuriated the Merkel government and was one of those agitating that the United States draw down troops from Germany—even as he took over the responsibilities of overseeing the entire Intelligence Community. Trump and Trump aides, including National Security Advisor Robert O'Brien, lied about why Trump fired Maguire, saying it had to do with limitations on how long he could serve in an acting capacity. (This was not the case.)

Politico, reporting on the Maguire-Pierson case, noted that it was part of a bigger effort on Trump's part to push out anyone not seen as loyal, a particularly disturbing series of events as an election loomed. A senior White House official had told Politico reporter Alex Ward: "Anyone from here on out that opposes POTUS will get fired." The fact that this was a known shift in policy within the administration was confirmed to me by more than two dozen senior officials. Politico cited Axios journalist Jonathan Swan as saying that Trump's team had "assembled detailed lists of disloyal government officials to oust and trusted pro-Trump people to replace them."

Particularly chilling to observers was the number of people who would then be in places, like the Pentagon or the Intelligence Community, who could help Trump implement plans to ensure he maintained his hold on the presidency, or who could quash potential threats to him.

Secretary of Defense Mark Esper was another victim of the purges. He, like Joint Chiefs of Staff chairman Milley, had been increasingly concerned about Trump's attitude toward the military, especially after the incident in Lafayette Park. But both men determined to stay because they saw bigger risks ahead, especially pertaining to the election and its aftermath. They wanted to ensure it was conducted fairly and without any attempt to misuse the military.

Esper recalled: "I felt at that point that [by November 2, 2020] I had given it my best, followed my game plan, kept my integrity, and made a difference. I had succeeded, and was prepared to leave after the election if that was my fate. I then spent another week at the Pentagon, which surprised me; and then the president fired me on November 9th. Because of the way he did it, the timing, and the lack of explanation, his action provoked its own firestorm of concerns as to what might be underway. Adding fuel to the fire was the fact that the president not only replaced me with an unknown person who used to work in the Trump White House, but also because they began firing other senior civilian officials at the Pentagon and replacing them with real loyalists. This really concerned a lot of folks both within the department and outside it.

"General Milley, of course, was now all alone by himself. There was no senior civilian he could trust to take the lead or provide top cover. On top of this, the chairman of the Joint

Chiefs of Staff has no command authority, an important fact that most people don't understand. He's an advisor to the secretary of the defense and to the president. It is the SecDef who possesses the authority to mobilize and deploy troops, and the chairman has no authority to do anything about it if he disagrees with a decision. For those who understood these authorities and dynamics, this became a point of concern as Trump loyalists moved into the Pentagon and the White House began a vigorous challenge to the election results."

Esper continued: "I was concerned for months that the president would flood the Pentagon with loyalists who would do harm to the institution and to our national security if I resigned. This was the major reason I chose not to do so, but at the same time worked to do my duty and sense of what's right without getting unnecessarily fired too soon. I just had no confidence the White House would bring in a serious professional, a leader, somebody who respected the institution and our commitments, and most importantly our oath of office. That's why my goal became getting to and through November 2nd, and letting the voters decide the future through a free and fair election."

As another senior Trump official present after the November election observed: "If good people don't join the administration to serve their country, then you're stuck with bad people. And you see at the end of the Trump administration, those last seventy days, bad people are really taking hold of some of the instruments of our government and what that can mean."

In the week after the election, Trump appointed multiple new top officials at the Pentagon. As acting secretary of defense he chose Christopher Miller, the director of the National Counterterrorism Center. "Chris will do a GREAT job! Mark Esper has been terminated," Trump tweeted.

Miller, although a respected counterterrorism professional and former special forces officer, created concerns at senior levels in the Pentagon because he had very little top Pentagon management experience. Also, making the shift during a presidential transition, when the president making the change had just lost the election, felt wrong. On Capitol Hill there were also concerns. Rep. Elissa Slotkin (D-MI) felt compelled to say at the time: "It is critical that he and all senior Pentagon leaders remember that they swore an oath to the Constitution, not any one man. With that oath comes a commitment to the peaceful transition of power. All leaders must decide what they will do in the next seventy-two days." Notably, Miller had been appointed over the person who by statute would have filled the acting role, Deputy Secretary of Defense David Norquist.

Colonel Douglas Macgregor, an extreme ideologue who would later be known for the seemingly pro-Russia tilt to his Fox News analyses of the Ukraine war, was named as a senior advisor to Miller. Another new presidential appointee was Michael Ellis as general counsel at the National Security Agency, despite the objections of the NSA director, General Paul Nakasone. Other people promoted to key Pentagon jobs at that time included three described by the *New York Times* as "highly ideological Trump foot soldiers": Kashyap Patel, Anthony Tata, and Ezra Cohen-Watnick. Patel was a former Devin Nunes staffer who had worked actively to discredit the stories of Russian interference in the elections. Tata had once called President Obama a terrorist.

One highly respected Republican national security specialist said: "[Chris Miller] ought to have had the self-respect to decline the offer. Because what was apparent, of him as acting secretary, is that he genuinely didn't understand how to do the job. For example, he gave an interview, I think, to the *New Yorker* and it was just hair raising. He accused people in the Pentagon of denying him information on nuclear planning, of not letting his people do the supervision. But the thing is, they didn't have the clearances for it. And so he assumed there was a plot against him, when in fact he just didn't understand how the system worked. And so one of the key failures of the Trump administration was putting decreasingly qualified people in senior positions and undermining the institutions' effectiveness as a result."

A senior State Department official observed that by the last three months of the Trump era: "You had a really bizarre collection of folks stuck in there. And if that was not bad enough, we really saw it as a sign of what was coming. That more would be coming."

Others were concerned that a cornered Trump, in the last days of his administration might take steps against the United States or against the world. Elizabeth Neumann said: "He was *this* close to corrupting the military. And you worry, at what point do the guardrails fall apart? And you carry that to one extreme and we make really bad foreign policy decisions, we end up in a war, or we make bad decisions about nuclear weapons. That would be catastrophic. But there's also this other side that I don't know that even in retrospect, we fully appreciate. But part of what convinced me to speak out was the Lafayette Square incident. I was worried we would have a point at which no one would stand up and object, to say to the president, 'You can't do that. That's not how this works. The federal government doesn't have the authority to do what you want us to do.' And then you flash forward to what happened on January 6th, and you're like, 'Oh, my gosh. We were not very far away from the institutions turning on the people in the United States.' It's frightening how quickly we got there."

Meanwhile, not only was Trump trying to remake the government so it would be more pliable, but also he was continuing to promote the Big Lie. He was actively meeting with advisors who were advocating everything from seizing voting machines to pushing fraudulent slates of electors. It became so extreme that even core advisors and enablers who had always fallen in line to support Trump, including in some of his worst initiatives, felt a line must be drawn. Attorney General William Barr resigned in December 2020 after announcing that his department had found no evidence of fraud in the election. In his book *One Damn Thing After Another* he asserted that by the end of his presidency Trump cared only about himself. In interviews Barr said that by that point Trump listened only to a "coterie of sycophants," went "off the rails," did "a lot of damage" by claiming the election was stolen and by helping to tee up the January 6 Capitol riot. (Barr also said he would vote again for Trump. He felt the progressive agenda pushed by Democrats was a greater threat to the country than a man who tried to subvert our democracy. So it is clear he did not undergo any great awakening in the light of Trump's extraordinary abuses, but rather that overthrowing the government was just a bridge too far for the two-time attorney general.)

Kori Schake recalled other steps taken to speak out as January 6 approached. Notably, there was a letter published on January 3, signed by all living secretaries of defense—from both parties—urging the military to stay out of domestic political disputes. Schake credits Rep. Liz Cheney (R-WY) with organizing the writing of the letter: "How did Liz Cheney know to orchestrate that? Because for four or five months, the military was thinking strategically about how to prevent themselves from being used by a president to prevent the peaceful transition of power. And the coordination that was going on with the congressional armed services members and everybody else. So that Congress stood in front of the military and defended them politically and kept them out of the fray was really important."

The letter was another example of how professionals from both parties could come together and, as recommended by the Transition Integrity Project, use public communications to mobilize public opinion as another guardrail to keep a rogue president in check. Signed by Ashton Carter, Dick Cheney, William Cohen, Mark Esper, Robert Gates, Chuck Hagel, James Mattis, Leon Panetta, William Perry, and Donald Rumsfeld, it began:

"As former secretaries of defense, we hold a common view of the solemn obligations of the U.S. armed forces and the Defense Department. Each of us swore an oath to support and defend the Constitution against all enemies, foreign and domestic. We did not swear it to an individual or a party."

It cited America's two-hundred-year history of peaceful transitions of power. It stated that "efforts to involve the U.S. armed forces in resolving election disputes would take us into dangerous, unlawful and unconstitutional territory." It specifically stated that Miller and his subordinates were "bound by oath, law and precedent to facilitate the entry into office of the incoming administration, and to do so wholeheartedly."

Clearly, they like so many others saw the handwriting on the wall. Trump had indicated as early as 2016 that he would challenge the legitimacy of any election he did not win. He had repeatedly demonstrated that neither the law nor standards of decency would limit his behavior. When obstacles were placed in front of him, he either ignored them or removed them. As many of his top aides had noted, he did not care about anything but himself—not the Constitution, not the country, not America's standing in the world, not the truth, not the law, not how history would someday remember him.

And that is why on January 6, 2020, he exhorted a mob to march to the Capitol. That is why he urged, pushed, and threatened his vice president to ignore his constitutional responsibilities—to at least temporarily not recognize the legitimate results of the election. This tactic would give Trump a chance to put in place alternative electors. Or to contest the results to the point that the House of Representatives would have to decide the outcome. He would be certain of winning because the vote would be by state delegation, and the GOP controlled the majority of state delegations (even though they were in the minority overall).

At that moment—as rioters carrying Trump banners assaulted the Capitol, with the ensuing melee leading to seven deaths and over 150 injuries to police officers—it was the professionalism of government officials who chose to respect the Constitution, rather than succumb to pressures from the president and those acting on his behalf, that stopped this wayward presidency in its death throes from derailing American democracy. Even though the guardrail held, however, it did not eliminate future risks to our system of government from Trump, or someone like him.

CHAPTER SEVEN

Bullets and Boomerangs

There is nothing wrong in America that can't be fixed
with what is right in America.

—BILL CLINTON

D WIGHT EISENHOWER ONCE said: "History does
not long entrust the care of freedom to the weak or
the timid." As it turns out, that's not always true.
Few American political leaders have earned a reputation for
dead-eyed passivity like Vice President Mike Pence. In the
course of writing this book, I have heard people who worked
with him and knew him well call him a "coward," an "empty
suit," "an HOV-lane inflatable dummy," and "Trump's abused
spouse." Some of these folks actually liked him. But no one
spoke of him as a strong leader.

Yet on January 6, 2020, in the face of immense pressure
and an angry mob, with history staring him square in the
eye, he had to make a choice that could determine the future
of democracy in America. He was, according to all reports,
uncertain what to do up until the last minute. But, in part

thanks to a phone call from Dan Quayle (another former Indiana vice president who himself was seen as something of a lightweight), when the stakes were highest Mike Pence did the right thing. (Pence and his advisors kept calling around seeking advice on this. Among those urging Pence to do as the law required was J. Michael Luttig, a judge who was something of a conservative icon. His views were folded into Pence's final statement on this matter.)

Before he did the right thing, Pence very nearly did the wrong thing. Trump wanted the vice president, who was to preside over the official certification of the electoral votes on January 6, to avoid doing so. Trump wanted Pence to say there were too many unresolved questions and to delay a final decision. According to multiple sources, Pence spent considerable time in December 2020 trying to find a way to do as Trump wanted. One person close to Pence told me: "He really seemed to believe that some of the election results were faulty. Or at least that is what he said as he tried to justify it."

Trump pushed him. The implication was that if Pence did not do this he would fall from grace, potentially imperiling his chances of someday succeeding Trump as president. On the morning of January 6, according to a report in the *New York Times*, Trump had a call with Pence in which he said: "You can either go down in history as a patriot or you can go down in history as a pussy." (Trump later confirmed this conversation took place.)

Finally, according to the Woodward-Costa book *Peril*, Pence called Dan Quayle. He laid out the case, asking for guidance. The authors report that Quayle saw the matter in black and white. The case was clear-cut. His advice was reportedly blunt: "Mike, you have no flexibility on this. None. Zero. Forget it. Put it away."

Even then Pence did not let the matter drop. He pushed Quayle, looking for a way to delay the process. Only after Quayle stood his ground did Pence relent.

While Trump's pressure continued, Pence formulated a plan. Perhaps it was out of a sense of right and wrong. Perhaps it was a political calculation. Perhaps there was a voice in his head that sounded a little like the bland Pennsylvania judge James Wilson in the musical *1776*. Presented with the opportunity to cast the vote that blocks independence, Wilson goes with the majority because, as he puts it: "I'm different from you, John [Dickinson, the Pennsylvania colleague pressing him to vote no]. I'm different from most of the men here. I don't want to be remembered." Part of Pence did not want to be seen as the man who defied 240 years of precedent to throw America into the biggest constitutional crisis it had faced since the Civil War.

Trump did not know which way Pence would go. When the president spoke to a crowd of supporters gathered on the Ellipse, the park a few hundred yards from the White House, he tried to use his bully pulpit to pressure the vice president one more time: "If Mike Pence does the right thing, we win the election. All Vice President Pence has to do is send it back to the states to recertify, and we become president and you are the happiest people."

Before he began the process of certifying the vote, Pence said in a statement that it was his "considered judgment that my oath to support and defend the Constitution constrains me from claiming unilateral authority to determine which electoral votes should be counted and which should not."

It was not a particularly heroic act. After all, Pence was simply following the established law and centuries of practice. There was no gray area, as Quayle had indicated. Had

Pence done as Trump asked, he would have been an active participant in sedition, an illegal attempt to subvert American democracy. But in the end he too was a guardrail. Whether it was the strength of his character or something less noble that motivated him to do the right thing, what he did made a difference.

It also inflamed the crowd of Trump's supporters whom the president had exhorted to march to the Capitol that day in an effort to influence or even stop the certification of the vote. They became angrier and angrier as the news of what Pence had done reached them. They built a gallows on the steps of the Capitol building and chanted: "Hang Mike Pence!"

When asked about this afterward, Trump said: "Well, the people were very angry." He also did nothing to calm the crowd of thousands as they grew ever more violent. He did not take any steps to demand they disperse. In fact, instead he punctuated his silence with a video in which he said: "We had an election that was stolen from us. It was a landslide election and everyone knows it, especially the other side." Far from condemning the actions of the mob who stormed the building, attacked police, searched for members of Congress forced to hide in their offices fearing for their lives, Trump's message to the insurrectionists was "We love you. You're very special."

The riot was, to paraphrase military theorist Carl Von Clausewitz, the continuation of the effort to undo the election using other means. If they could not do it via process, they would try to do it via force. Although the riot was eventually quashed, the day continues to reverberate in American politics. Despite the fact that Trump's plans failed and he was roundly repudiated, and the events of January 6 led him to become the only president in American history to be impeached twice, Trump and many in the GOP have continued to foster the themes that sparked the melee: the election was "stolen" and Trump should still be president.

On January 6 and in the days immediately after, that such themes could survive more than a few weeks would have been unthinkable. For a few brief hours in the aftermath of the attempted coup, there was unanimity about the horror of what had happened. Some in the GOP, like House minority leader Kevin McCarthy, had called Trump to plead with him to call off the mob. Sean Hannity of Fox did the same. While McCarthy would later change his tune, Senate minority leader Mitch McConnell did not. He condemned the attack when it happened, calling for law enforcement authorities to investigate it. (Yet he voted against convicting Trump in the second impeachment.) On the first anniversary of the attack he called it "horrendous," described it as a "violent insurrection," and laid responsibility for it firmly at the president's door, saying it was "provoked by Trump."

Following the attack, top Trump administration officials resigned in protest. This wasn't especially heroic. They had just a few more days left in office anyway. Many DC insiders were amazed their consciences had allowed them to stay so long. They included Betsy DeVos, the education secretary and a Trump stalwart; Elaine Chao, the transportation secretary and McConnell's wife; acting secretary of homeland security Chad Wolf; Mick Mulvaney, the former White House chief of staff who at the time of the rioting had been serving as special envoy to Northern Ireland; Deputy National Security Advisor Matthew Pottinger; the First Lady's chief of staff Stephanie Grisham (who would later write, like many former Trump officials, an extremely condemnatory book about the president); a deputy White House press secretary; the acting chairman of the White House Council of Economic Advisers;

and multiple senior officials from various agencies as well as from the National Security Council and White House staff.

DeVos called the events of January 6, 2021, "unconscionable for our country." Chao said the events "deeply troubled me in a way that I simply cannot set aside." Wolf called them "tragic and sickening," although like many of the other senior Trump officials who stepped down he stopped short of ascribing to the president his fair share of blame. Mulvaney said: "I can't do it. I can't stay." Grisham in her book said Trump watched the attack on the Capitol gleefully and would hit rewind, viewing it over and over again.

The issue of when and whether to resign had haunted many Trump staffers from the day they first contemplated accepting their job. Some argued that by staying they could limit the damage done by the president, and where possible ensure good was done. But, often, quitting was the best way to draw attention to an issue, and to maintain one's integrity rather than undertake a task that was illegal or damaging to the national interest.

Chris Liddell, who served as deputy White House chief of staff, was highly thought of by his colleagues. He avoided controversy and was regarded as an asset who smoothed the functioning of the White House on the occasions it actually functioned. Deeply troubled by what happened on January 6, in his distress he began to reach out to friends and colleagues. One even said he was in tears. Reportedly, he was torn. He wanted to quit. But he was also concerned about what might happen in the White House in the remaining days of the president's term. One colleague, Josh Bolten, the former White House chief of staff, said: "I told him he needed to stay. There was a transition going on. And there needed to be a sane person who would speak for the White House periodically, as long as Trump wasn't aware of it, and make sure that the right things still happened." Another former White House staffer recounted a similar story: "He wasn't the only one. But, you know, he didn't have to stay. He had plenty of money from his previous life. The White House was a horror show at the time. And yet a sense of duty matters. And some good work did get done, although Trump did everything in his power to downplay and even obstruct the transition."

One of those who decided to resign was Christopher Ford. Like Esper, he had long planned to step down. Unlike Esper, he was not forced out by Trump but rather by events. Ford told me: "I had wanted to leave gracefully in January 2021. I had submitted my letter of resignation on January 4, to become effective just before Joe Biden's inauguration day. That, I thought, would give me time to properly brief the Biden transition team and get my own paperwork in order as I headed out the door. I also wanted to do what I could to protect my outstanding staff from any weird, last-minute retaliation that might occur before our administration walked out the door. But then the sixth of January happened, and though I didn't watch any TV that day and only caught up on the coverage the next morning, it was pretty clear how close America had come to a real catastrophe. Over the course of the next morning, it became clear to me that things were now on a whole new level, and I no longer had the option of walking out in a 'normal,' decorous sort of way.

"In any administration, you basically need to have in your head some idea of what you won't do, what lines you won't cross, what sort of things will lead to you resign on the spot. In the Trump administration, there had occasionally been things that walked up to that line for me, things within my WMD-related portfolio that I can't talk about, where if we had gone any further down a particular road, I would have been out the door immediately. But they didn't happen. Yet January 6th did. This wasn't just crazy talk. This was a violent effort to seize our national legislature in order to stop the US Constitution from functioning and to overthrow a national election, undertaken on the basis of a gleefully encouraged lie. Jesus. I had already sent my letter of resignation and by the morning of January 7th had even already sent out an email to my staff to express how impressed and amazed and grateful I was to have worked with these national security professionals, and to give them the appreciation that I felt they deserved—and they weren't getting from anybody else in the administration, which neither liked nor trusted the national security professionals that the American taxpayer pays to keep us safe. But January 6th really changed everything.

"As I was catching up on the news on January 7, I was basically wigging out. I've been a law and order Republican all my life, and all of us in government had sworn to uphold the US Constitution. There was no way anyone who took that oath seriously could countenance the attack on the Capitol. So, I resubmitted my letter of resignation the next day, and I made it effective immediately. And I walked out of the building on the eighth. I didn't feel there was any alternative. To be fair, I don't pretend that this was a tremendously costly personal decision, for I was obviously already planning to leave in a couple of weeks anyway. But I was bowled over by how fucking godawful the sixth was, and I couldn't remain a part of the team any longer. So it was goodbye."

In the immediate aftermath of the attack on the Capitol, members of Congress began to again call for Trump's impeachment. By January 8, 110 members of Congress had signed on to articles of impeachment drafted by Democrats

Rep. David Cicilline of Rhode Island, Rep. Ted Lieu of California, and Rep. Jamie Raskin of Maryland. The number of supporters had nearly doubled by the eleventh, when an article of impeachment was introduced in the House of Representatives. With so much support, the article was assured of passage and by the twelfth, less than a week after the attack, the impeachment process began. On the thirteenth, a week after the attack, Trump was impeached. All Democrats in the House supported the action, as did ten Republicans, including a member of the Republican House leadership and the daughter of a former Republican vice president, Rep. Liz Cheney of Wyoming.

The Senate trial did not begin until after Trump had left office, but was considered worth pursuing. Had he been convicted, he would have been barred from seeking elected office again. Forty-eight Democrats and seven Republicans voted to convict, ten votes short of the two-thirds majority needed. But the vote was historic, the most bipartisan of its kind in US history. (Such votes often fall along very partisan lines.)

When I spoke to the authors of the articles of impeachment, they made it clear the process was pursued for several reasons. One was the gravity of the crime. Another was the concern of many that Trump might become even more erratic and dangerous in his final weeks in office. (Echoing this, on January 8 for the second time in three months, General Milley had called the Chinese to say he would let them know if the United States was going to attack China. This was a step he characterized in congressional testimony as "deconfliction." He said his call had been "generated by concerning intelligence which caused us to believe the Chinese were worried about an attack by the US.") Finally, there was the issue of ruling out a Trump second term.

Speaking specifically to the issue of whether impeachment was an effective check, an example of the system working, Representative Lieu said: "I actually believe the impeachment power worked as intended. In both cases, the House impeached the former president, and it was actually two separate congresses that impeached him. The power to convict was lacking in the Senate. But I think the impeachment power in the House worked as intended."

Lieu continued: "I also think Abraham Lincoln had it right when he said, 'Public sentiment is everything: with it nothing can fail, without it, nothing can succeed.' Most people don't pay that much attention to politics. They're busy, they're living their lives, so impeachment caused a lot more people to focus on the corruption happening in the Trump administration. The public may wonder, 'Well, why is the president even being impeached?' And I think that in the case of the first impeachment, we saw more people paying attention to the bad things Trump was doing. His electoral prospects weren't why we impeached Trump, but it did help lead to the defeat of the incumbent president, which historically is hard. Incumbent presidents win. One of the reasons that Congressmen David Cicilline, Jamie Raskin, and I wrote the articles of impeachment a second time, while we were under lockdown, is that we didn't know what other crazy things he could do in between January 6th and January 20th. He still had fourteen days left, and so in our minds not only do we need to hold him accountable and get him out of office as soon as possible, but also we could have this impeachment hanging over him, and launch it to the Senate. And then he would know that if he did anything remotely crazier, he would be removed immediately."

Raskin, a constitutional scholar, put the action in a historical context: "The current shape of presidential power is a total prostitution of the constitutional design. And Trump tried to compound that, to make it even worse. There's a reason Congress is the Article I branch. Congress is designed to be the representatives of the people. And if you look at the powers of Congress, they're expansive, almost comprehensive. I mean, we have the power to regulate commerce domestically and internationally. We have the power to declare war. We have the power to raise armies and maintain navies. We have the power to raise taxes and to spend money, and so on. And then you get to the executive branch in Article II, with four short sections. The fourth section is about how you impeach a president who commits treason, bribery, or other high crimes and misdemeanors. But the core job of the president is to take care that the laws are faithfully executed. And there's a reason we can impeach the president and he can't impeach us. The people are sovereign here."

Raskin added: "You know, the role of the president came after. It didn't exist in the Articles of Confederation or the article of association that was added afterwards. It was a gesture towards executive efficiency and keeping things going on when Congress was not in town. But now everything has been capsized and just turned on its head, and the president is somehow deemed to be something like a king of the world. And it is an absurd departure from the basic constitutional understandings the framers had. We were conceived in insurgency against monarchical power."

He made one other salient observation: "There's a lot of nonsense about checks and balances in public understanding and political consciousness. The phrase 'checks and balances' doesn't appear anywhere in the Constitution. If you do a search for it in the Federalist Papers, the only place it appears is in the juxtaposition of the House and the Senate against each other. In a democratic society *people* are the check and the balance—the idea of a civic equality and each person having a voice in government. Combine that with respect for the rule of law and the Constitution and the democratic system does work. For example, during the election a lot of the people who stood up were county or state election officials. Like [Georgia secretary of state] Brad Raffensberger [who pushed back on Trump's efforts for him to find extra votes so Trump could win Georgia's electoral votes].

"That was a product of federalism, and the fact that there are also state governments that are not directly controlled by the federal government. And there were lots of people in the public, in the government, who stood up to Donald Trump along the way and a lot of it, in my mind, reflects constitutional patriotism. Colonel Vindman is a good example. I mean, these are people who felt that they swore an oath not to one guy, but to a system of constitutional values. And that belief in constitutional democracy itself is the sustaining ethos."

We Have Crossed the Rubicon

Former ambassador Jim Jeffrey, who has spent a lifetime in service in the military and the State Department, described the events of January 6 and the efforts by Trump and his supporters to undermine faith in our elections by saying: "The most dramatic thing that's happened in American life, certainly in my lifetime, has been the decision by a very significant part of the Republican Party, and the Republican base, to overthrow the core precept of democracy, which is not elections, but the fact that all elections are going to be contested and are going to be political and emotional. And, therefore, you have to have a system to decide who wins, who loses, just like in a football game: umpires and rules. And it was all driven by Trump; nobody else did this. We have crossed that Rubicon, with Trump and much of the Republican Party, and I'm very worried about my country."

Former defense secretary Esper said: "The institutions held, but too many of our leaders did not. By that I'm referring to any number of senior executive branch officials and members of Congress. Individuals failed at critical points, particularly after the election, while too few stood tall. Once the result of the election was ascertained in November, and credible concerns about election fraud were evaluated and dismissed, that should have been it. Republicans should have pressed the president to concede and help the Biden team transition. But most didn't, and that was a clear lack of leadership. Now I'm concerned that a large segment of the Republican base considers the 2020 presidential election as fraudulent and President Biden as illegitimate. That's a problem for our democracy."

He continued: "January 6th was a horrible and tragic day that will resonate darkly for a long time. The Capitol is such an important symbol of our democracy—the world's oldest and most respected republic—and the events of that day made clear that this gift from our Founding Fathers is more fragile than we realized. And so the violent insurrection that occurred on January 6th did not just hurt individuals caught up in the events of that day, it undermined America's standing in the world, as well as our moral authority to speak out about human rights, civil liberties, and democracy. And let's be honest, President Trump was responsible for what happened that day."

As she reflected on the events of January 6, former ambassador Marie Yovanovitch started by chiding herself. "I feel

like I was so naive," she said, "that every day I am so surprised
to hear how organized it was. There was a real conspiracy to
undermine the results of the election and our constitutional
order. And it was led by the president of the United States and
those closest to him. And as a foreign policy person, of course
it makes me think of everything I have seen overseas. And
one of the things I have written about is that Ukraine, which
is a subject of much criticism and sometimes ridicule, most recently managed their presidential transitions more peacefully
and far better than we did ours. And so what does that tell
you about the state of our democracy? It's sobering."

All the people with whom I spoke for this book shared a
view that something profound happened, not just on January 6, but during the four years of the Trump administration.
Some associated it with long-term decay they traced back decades in American politics: heightened polarization, incivility,
the elevation of the presidency into a nearly kingly position.
Some associated it with a darker turn taken when Trump took
over the Republican Party, introducing overt racism, disrespect for the rule of law, and authoritarian impulses.

But much as virtually everyone with whom I spoke shared
their concerns about these trends and the state of American
politics and governance, almost all those who had served directly in the Trump administration had another concern.

Rather than having dodged a bullet with Joe Biden's election, they felt we had only temporarily "dodged a boomer-
ang." Something could still come back and hit us. They were
concerned that Trump was still the leader of the Republican
Party, still committed to winning back the office he felt was
unjustly taken from him. They felt that should he regain the
presidency, his prior experience would lead him to quickly
finish the job he had started once he began to understand how

the US government worked. He would undertake a purge and ensure that in every critical position that could impact his ability to carry out his initiatives, whims, and desires, government officials would be appointed—above all else—because they were loyal to him. He would eradicate the impediments he had encountered to realizing his plans.

This concern has since been frequently justified by Trump's actions since he left office, by the rallies and interviews that are part of his permanent campaign, or what he would like the world to see as his presidency in exile. In March of 2022, he gave a speech at a rally in Florence, South Carolina, in which he said: "We will pass critical reforms making every executive branch employee fireable by the president of the United States. The deep state must and will be brought to heel."

Out of context, this might seem like a pretty arcane topic to bring up at a populist rally. But for Trump it was a top priority because it would effectively change the structure of the government in a fundamental way. All executive branch employees would serve at the pleasure of the president. All would therefore be beholden to him. Their first loyalty would effectively no longer be to the Constitution, but to him. And whistleblowers, aides with a different point of view, those who sought to stop him from violating the law or undermining US national security would, the moment such a regulation was passed, be silenced.

This was the direction in which Trump was heading during the last couple of years of his presidency. He saw loyal government officials, whom he derided as being members of the deep state, as an existential threat. They stood between him and the kind of foreign-dictator authoritarian rule he wanted to emulate.

ICHAEL ATKINSON, THE former inspector general of the Intelligence Community, described the threat this way: "I was interviewed by the White House counsel's office to become the inspector general before the president appointed me, and it was a very serious process. And the questions that were asked to me by the White House counsel's office—and this was summer of 2017—were 'Can you be independent? Give us examples of your independence. Can you be objective? Give us examples of your objectivity.' And I can't imagine in another Trump administration a similar vetting process for inspectors general. I think the questions would be the opposite. 'Can you not be objective? Can you not be independent, despite what the law requires? Can you give us examples where you're required to be independent, and you did something, where you carried someone else's water?' That's what I would expect of the vetting process. You know the question 'Who watches the watchers?' In a second Trump administration, they will know the ones who watch the watchers, and they will not bring in people who watch objectively, independently. I firmly believe that."

General James Clapper described a parallel worry regarding the placement of loyalists in Intelligence Community leadership: "The IC could pretty much withstand the pressure for four years of Trump. I don't think the country fully appreciates what Dan Coats did. He provided top cover for the IC, and held the line on the IC mantra of "Truth to Power," ultimately at the cost of his job. But if President Trump were reelected, it could be very damaging to the IC, and for that matter, other institutions of our government. The Intelligence Community organization which suffered the most during the Trump administration was the office I formerly headed,

ODNI. If that had continued into a second Trump term, it would have been pretty devastating."

Jim Jeffrey not only served Trump, but also believes some of Trump's foreign policy was effective. He has had no hesitation in defending those parts, but he worried that in a second term: "He would have people who were even more Trumpists than Trump. And their goal would be to get gold stars from Trump. So rather than a bureaucracy that was serving the country and sometimes challenging him, you would have one that would be assisting his every effort, creating faits accomplis. That would have made things worse than they were. It would have been disastrous. And, as you know, around January 6th there were signs we had come close to that in DOD, in places where they may have looked the other way and thereby enabled the riot on Capitol Hill."

Miles Taylor felt that had there been a second term the president would have bypassed seeking the consent of Congress and that "more than half the cabinet would be in 'acting' roles from the get-go," and there would be very little Congress could have done about it. "[Trump] would have been delighted in making that happen."

Veterans of jobs at the highest levels in both Republican and Democratic administrations spoke of other areas in which the further realization of a Trumpian vision would be grievously damaging. A former top Bush White House official cited senators and congressmen who were "derelict in their responsibility" to stand up to the president and defend the Constitution. He observed that Trump is deeply feared within the GOP. He is seen as someone who controls a critical group of voters and is actively trying to cull the GOP ranks of anyone who has ever criticized him. Another former

Republican cabinet official illustrated this point when he said: "Kevin McCarthy cares only about becoming Speaker of the House. He will ride with Trump as long as he has to and do whatever he has to to win that job." Andy Card warned of the breakdown in the functioning of the White House if the chief of staff were to be "more like the head of a political office than someone who is the right hand of the president." He added: "If the occupant of the Oval Office doesn't want a chief of staff, if there is no discipline, if there is no management" then "chaos and worse are the inevitable result."

Fiona Hill said: "I was deeply, deeply worried by everything else that was happening as I watched the end game. I just thought, 'These guys have lost it.' There were so many people who were just there for their own venal, tarnished personal agendas. And then there were people like Kash Patel and Chris Miller who stepped into positions way beyond their qualifications and experience. I was so deeply disappointed with all of these people who thought they could get themselves something out of being in Trump's orbit. It's just deeply troubling, because I think a lot of people lost a sense of themselves, and what they were there for—to serve the country, not the man or their own ambition. And I know that if Trump had been reelected that problem would only have gotten much, much worse."

The Central Challenge Confronting America Today

Rep. Jamie Raskin summed up the threat implicit in these comments and in a possible second Trump term. With the clarity of someone who has spent a quarter of a century as a professor of constitutional law at American University's Washington College of Law, framing his thoughts within a broader theory of government, he said:

"The history of authoritarianism is always the story of a would-be dictator or tyrant trying to step outside of the official constitutional structure and instead create a parallel shadow government. Sometimes it exists with the unleashing of vigilante paramilitaries, to go along with the official military and police. But it also involves creating bureaucratic back channels and political apparatuses that essentially mock and supplant the legitimate governmental structure. So that is the central worry: that there will be a president who will use his power essentially to purge the constitutional system of legitimacy and replace it with handpicked people who will not comply with the laws as passed by Congress, but instead just follow like robots the will of the president."

As we spoke, Raskin paused for a moment and then gravely added: "This is a very serious problem, the central challenge confronting American democracy today. The GOP under Donald Trump's thumb has positioned itself outside the constitutional order. It does not accept the basic norms of constitutional democracy. It does not accept the rule of law or the concept of majority rule. And it does not accept elections that don't favor Donald Trump. So that's a very dangerous combination of elements challenging our constitutional order."

The problem is compounded by the political era in which we live. Former ambassador Tom Shannon said to me: "We're going to be as divided as we are for quite some time. And in such an environment, the big question is how do you make government work knowing that in our system today politicization is like water, that it knows no natural boundary." He emphasized the importance of erecting those boundaries. He

noted how important it is that future leaders spend time in-
culcating in career Foreign Service Officers—and the military, civil servants, and intelligence officers—that on the job
they are not and cannot be Democrats or Republicans. They
do not serve one individual, but rather the Constitution and
the people of the United States.

Shannon's vision, honed after decades spent in the Foreign Service, is that public service must be a calling and a
profession. The ideal he offered up is not only what the government should be about, but also what it *must* be about if it is
to both function successfully and serve all Americans equally.
He said that over and over, through the years "I've counseled
young Foreign Service Officers about what it means to be an
American diplomat as opposed to a Democratic diplomat or
Republican diplomat. That it was our job to accept the will
of the American people as expressed through our institutions
and our Constitution. It was our job to try to make government work, and to ensure that the newly elected leadership
could have confidence in the institutions they were inheriting,
so they didn't do harm to institutions. But that we also had an
obligation to defend those institutions and in the end, above
all, to do what was right. And that was all fine in theory, but
I knew then, and it is clearer to me more than ever today, that
this is a tough assignment, and it is going to get tougher."

How do we ensure that attitude prevails when there is a
movement afoot in our country to undermine those views, to
implicitly rewrite the Pledge of Allegiance to make it about
an individual or a particular party? As Mark Zaid the whistleblower lawyer said: "There are certainly many laws and
regulations that the Congress can strengthen. There are procedures that we can encourage people to follow. But at the
end of the day, it's still going to come down to the character

and the strength of conviction of the individuals we place in critical jobs—not just jobs at the top of government, but at every level, because the government is so big and so much of significance takes place at so many levels within it."

One lesson of the Trump years, though, is that once again as has been the case throughout American history—from our fragile formative years through a great civil war, from our emergence as a global power to the predation of a corrupt president sponsored by a foreign enemy—our society has regularly surprised the world. We have managed to do so because of the genius of our Constitution and our respect for the law. We have done so because our politics have evolved over time and our system, deeply flawed and inequitable for so many from the start, has been designed to evolve, and our leaders have taken advantage of that design. We have done so because, being an open society, when our policymakers were not wise their mistakes were identified and corrected, either by their own hand or at the ballot box. And to a much greater extent than many understand, we have survived because of the seriousness of purpose and dedication of the professionals within our government.

The question we must ask now is, can that legacy be carried forward? Or will the authoritarian thugs who have attacked the foundations of our democracy disable the most critical mechanisms of our government, the fail-safes and guardrails, the guides and values that ensure it works as intended—and that when it does not, they draw attention to what is dysfunctional and ensure its repair.

Democracy, as it turns out, is about more than the ballot box. It is about systems that ensure we are never answerable to one individual or a faction, that we are, as John Adams hoped, "a nation of laws and not of men." That means that not just presidents or elected officials are empowered by our government. By taking an oath to serve the Constitution, all who work at the many levels of our federal, state, and local governments also serve the people, and as was so well articulated by Representative Raskin, the ideals of constitutional patriotism.

In this book I have recorded the views of some of those who battled to defend those principles—not always well, not necessarily consistently, sometimes only after they had made grave errors—in the face of the criminal abuses and dangerous impulses of the most corrupt president in American history. My goal has been not only to give them credit for their courage and service but also, more importantly, to help provide a better understanding of some of the invisible checks and balances within our system. Also, by cataloguing some of the internal threats America faced and understanding what helped to mitigate them, I hope we can consider ways to strengthen what might be considered the immune system of the US government: the processes by which we protect ourselves from threats within our body politic.

I am under no illusions. This book has not been comprehensive. Indeed, we are daily exposed to new revelations about the extent of the abuses committed by former president Trump and the loyalists who surrounded him. Further, it is impossible to know the full number of people who just by doing their jobs might have played a role in the American resistance movement—a movement that protected us in moments of grave threats to our national security, our public health, our system of laws, and our democracy. I have no doubt that by hearing and heeding their stories we could emerge stronger and better able to repel future threats.

But I have felt it especially important to prepare this book now, incomplete though it may be, because we remain at a moment of great national peril. The risks that manifested themselves during the four years of the Trump administration have not abated. Despite the profound shock associated with Trump's worst abuses—from the betrayal of the country to foreign enemies, to efforts to weaken our most critical alliances; from attempts to further institutionalize racism and xenophobia in America, to the negligence leading to hundreds of thousands of needless deaths during the pandemic; from seeking to gut our institutions and laws to effectively ending our centuries-old democracy—the people and impulses behind those threats not only remain but in some cases have grown stronger.

It is not out of the question that in the years ahead, Trump or others like him will again gain high office. They may pervert the powers granted them in order to place themselves above the law. They may try to ensure that the greed, ambition, and views of a narrow minority prevail over the aspirations and values of the majority. It may be necessary, then, that the memory of our recent past—the moments people of character, courage, and a sense of duty defused or defeated significant dangers—serve not only as a cautionary tale, but also perhaps as a manual, a field guide, to preserving American democracy.

I wish it were not so. But I am afraid it is.

Having said that, as the stories within these pages reveal, we may take some comfort from the fact that the ranks of the good and the honest and decent within every branch of the US government vastly outnumber those who might pose a threat. That is the role they have played for generations. The result is that our institutions not only remain strong, but also will likely remain so for generations to come.

Acknowledgments

All books are collaborations. This is especially true of books that seek to fairly present the voice of a large, diverse professional community. It is impossible of course to be comprehensive in such circumstances. But thanks to the support of an extraordinary group of men and women who assisted with the preparation of *American Resistance,* I feel readers will get a sense of the way Washington works and how well served we were during a time of crisis and challenge. A large number of people became heroes by "just doing their jobs"—Democrats, Republicans, Independents, Foreign Service Officers, civil servants, military leaders, members of the intelligence community, elected officials, and others.

First, I must thank you, my editor on this book, Clive Priddle. He and his colleagues at PublicAffairs and Hachette have been smart, patient, supportive, and also patient as this book made its way from idea to reality. I have worked with Clive on two other books, *Running the World: The Inside Story of the National Security Council and the Architects of American Power* and *National Insecurity: American Leadership in an Age of Fear.* He has been such a good friend and a genuine pleasure to talk with about almost everything, that this book was as much a product of wanting to find another project to do with him as it was anything else. It also, I hope, fits with the other two books by providing insights into the behind-the-scenes workings of power (and intrigue and public service) in Washington. I hope there are more such books to come, and plan to submit them on time. I really, really do.

I was introduced to Clive very nearly two decades ago by my agent, Esmond Harmsworth. It is deeply disturbing to me that during that time they have not aged, while I on the other hand have become their portrait of Dorian Gray. Perhaps that is why they still work with me. In any event, I am grateful for the opportunity, regardless of the reason. Esmond not only is a great agent, but also a great friend. He has been a terrific guide from whom I have learned much over all these many years.

I also would like to thank my colleagues at TRG Media, the DSR Network, and *Deep State Radio* for providing the inspiration for this book and, on a weekly basis, a job that is pretty much ideal. I get to speak with some of the most brilliant people in the world about topics of greatest interest to me. TRG's chairman, Bernard L. Schwartz, the wisest and most optimistic person I know, has made it all possible. He has dedicated his life to many of the ideals enumerated in this book, and I learn from him every time we speak. My colleagues on the management side at TRG, Chris Cotnoir, Grant Haver— and during the first phases of this project, Stacy Williams (who now works in the US government)—have been hugely helpful with this book, as they are with everything else we try to do at our company. Grant, in particular, came to play a vital role on this book and I think it is fair to say that without his tireless efforts, completing it in any reasonable time frame would have been impossible. I'm deeply indebted to him for stepping up and for his energy, intelligence, and good advice throughout the process.

Deep State Radio, our flagship podcast, began in 2017. It would not have been created, nor would it have flourished as it has, without the creativity and brilliance of our guests. First that of Rosa Brooks and Kori Schake, who have long been the anchors of our conversations; and almost immediately thereafter that of Ed Luce and David Sanger. There have been many other exceptional guests on the program, and many of our conversations helped to shape this book and the ideas within it. Being the host of *DSR* is like always being in graduate school, but only with the very best, most interesting teachers. To each and every guest let me say that you were the best one, the most enjoyable, and the only reason I am not identifying you by name is that I don't want to make anyone else feel bad.

If you have come this far in the book, you now realize that at its core have been many interviews. Many. I tried to count them in my head, but suffice it to say there are at least one hundred. Of these, many of the interviews were off the record or on background, and so I am unable to cite the individuals with whom I spoke. Often this is because they still serve in the government. To each of those to whom this applies, I want to thank you, not just for your assistance with this small volume but for your ongoing service to this country. Among those I can cite and to whom I am deeply grateful are Michael Atkinson, Josh Bolton, Andy Card, Michael Chertoff, General James Clapper, Mark Esper, Dr. Anthony Fauci, Christopher Ford, Fiona Hill, James Jeffrey, Rep. Ted Lieu, Elaine McCusker, Michael McKinley, Elizabeth Neumann, Kirstjen Nielsen, Leon Panetta, Rep. Jamie Raskin, former ambassador Tom Shannon, Miles Taylor, former ambassador William Taylor, Olivia Troye, Lt. Col. Alexander Vindman, former ambassador Marie Yovanovitch, and Mark Zaid. All of you, cited and uncited, provided massively more great material than could be used in one book. And you reminded me why I do this. It's not the late, lonely nights writing and editing, believe me. It is the chance to meet with and listen to and be inspired by and learn from people like everyone who gave their time to help.

Many others—guests on the show, guests on panels on which I've appeared, people I have known for years in and around Washington, faculty at universities where I have spoken, and other journalists—have also been helpful by providing insights, tidbits, and needed perspective. I am grateful to you all.

That said, as the dedication to this book makes clear, each and every thing I do in my life is for my family. They are a constant source of joy and inspiration, needed humor, vital grounding, and, well, the best times of my life. That includes my sister and brother and their families. It includes my parents, who though both are gone, are the ones whose approval I continue to seek by writing these books. And it also includes my wonderful in-laws Stoil and Margarita Dirlikov.

My daughters, Joanna and Laura, are the lights of my life. They have exceeded in every respect my highest hopes for them and have taught me everything worth knowing in life. (Also some things not worth knowing . . . like, you know, how to navigate the Twitterverse. But I love them so wholly and completely that even things like that are forgiven.) I am also absolutely delighted that each of them has found a truly wonderful man to be with. Brad Becker-Parton and Aaron Nemo have upped the collective game of our family in myriad ways, and they too are a source of great joy. I love them all.

Finally, it is fair to say that when it comes to my remarkable, brilliant, patient, inspiring wife, Carla, I must begin by saying nothing I ever do, this book included, would be possible without her. But, honestly, I would not want to do any of it without her. She has made every day we have been together the best kind of adventure. She has made me see the world as I had never seen it before, and has expanded my horizons in countless ways. Along with her trusty sidekick, Grizzly (who has also served as director of research on this project, despite his inability to read, his disinclination to learn how to write, and his preference for spending all his time sleeping and eating), she makes every moment of my life worth living. I love her with all my heart.

Thanks to you all, and let's do this again sometime soon. Not right now, perhaps. But soon.

Index

CHRISTOPHER LEAMAN

David Rothkopf is an author and commentator specializing in foreign policy, national security, and politics. He was a senior official in the Clinton administration, CEO and editor of *Foreign Policy* magazine, and he has taught international affairs at Columbia University/SIPA, Georgetown University/SFS, and Johns Hopkins/SAIS. He is the author of many books, including *Running the World, National Insecurity, Superclass, Power, Inc., Great Questions of Tomorrow,* and most recently *Traitor: A History of American Betrayal from Benedict Arnold to Donald Trump.* He is host of the podcast *Deep State Radio* and is CEO of TRG Media. He is also a columnist for The Daily Beast, a member of the board of contributors for *USA Today,* and has written for numerous leading publications and appeared on leading broadcast networks worldwide.

PublicAffairs is a publishing house founded in 1997. It is a tribute to the standards, values, and flair of three persons who have served as mentors to countless reporters, writers, editors, and book people of all kinds, including me.

I. F. Stone, proprietor of *I. F. Stone's Weekly*, combined a commitment to the First Amendment with entrepreneurial zeal and reporting skill and became one of the great independent journalists in American history. At the age of eighty, Izzy published *The Trial of Socrates*, which was a national bestseller. He wrote the book after he taught himself ancient Greek.

Benjamin C. Bradlee was for nearly thirty years the charismatic editorial leader of *The Washington Post*. It was Ben who gave the *Post* the range and courage to pursue such historic issues as Watergate. He supported his reporters with a tenacity that made them fearless and it is no accident that so many became authors of influential, best-selling books.

Robert L. Bernstein, the chief executive of Random House for more than a quarter century, guided one of the nation's premier publishing houses. Bob was personally responsible for many books of political dissent and argument that challenged tyranny around the globe. He is also the founder and longtime chair of Human Rights Watch, one of the most respected human rights organizations in the world.

• • •

For fifty years, the banner of Public Affairs Press was carried by its owner Morris B. Schnapper, who published Gandhi, Nasser, Toynbee, Truman, and about 1,500 other authors. In 1983, Schnapper was described by *The Washington Post* as "a redoubtable gadfly." His legacy will endure in the books to come.

Peter Osnos, *Founder*